How to make people do what you want & How to change your mind

Christopher Rothchester

Table of Contents

How to Make People Do What You Want 5

Introduction 6

Chapter 1: Develop Balanced Self Confidence.......................7

Chapter 2: Persuasive Techniques, First Impressions, and 20

Chapter 3: Empathy.......................34

Chapter 4: How to be Pleasant to be Around 48

Chapter 5: Understanding Psychology 60

Conclusion.......................74

How To Change Your Mindset and Rewire your Brian 98

Introduction 99

Chapter 1: Using Neuroplasticity to Success.......................101

Chapter 2: A Winner's Belief System 112

Chapter 3: Turn a Negative Into a Positive.......................124

Chapter 4: Growth Mindsets Vs. Fixed Mindsets 134

Chapter 5: How To Connect The Brain and Soul to Gain.......... 145

Chapter 6: Natural Brain Detoxes and How Sleep Is a Key 155

Chapter 7: A List of Advanced Mindfulness and Meditation 164

Chapter 8: Formulating a Strategy 173

Chapter 9: Wandering Mind - DMN/TPN Mode, and How To.. 186

Chapter 10: ADHD - Deep Look Into the ADHD Brain in 194

RESOURCES: 206

How to Make People Do What You Want

Influence Human Behavior to Persuade
People and Win Friends

Christopher Rothchester

Introduction

Congratulations on purchasing How to Make People Do What You Want, and I thank you heartily for doing so.

Whenever I start reading a book and it begins with an introduction outlining everything in detail that I'm about to read about, I think: "Just let me find that out when I read it!" So I will spare you the burden of hearing some long description of what you are about to read. Suffice it to say that I prepared this book with care, with you in mind, your future, your happiness, and I earnestly hope that through these pages I can help you in some way. The following chapters will discuss how to overcome yourself to reach your full potential. In order to be a charismatic, pleasant, happy person, you may need to overcome some habits. When we change how we think, we change who we are, we become a new person. No, you don't need to forget who you are and lose your personality, you just need to control your own life rather than letting someone or something else rule you. None of us want to be slaves or be imprisoned, but how do you escape a prison or slavery that you don't know you're in? You can't! So you have to become aware of what is influencing your life and hindering your ability to accomplish your goals. To be truly free, limitless, powerful, and loving, you need to know yourself well. This book will show you how to understand how you think and how to relate to others. I truly hope this may propel you forward in the road of life.

There are plenty of books on this subject out there, and I honestly doubt that my humble skill has produced the best one by any means, but I do hope this may be a good start for you. Thanks again for choosing my little book! Now let's begin...

Chapter 1: Develop Balanced Self Confidence

How do you feel about yourself? Your answer to this question will affect how you deal with others and how you treat yourself. Some people think too much of themselves and others think too little; balance can be hard to find. I have experienced both at different times.

At first, quite a few years ago, I used to overestimate my abilities, but after failing to achieve my expectations a few times, I was put in my place. Then I began to underestimate myself, fearing failure around every corner. Eventually, I found that none of the things I feared ever seemed to happen, as I usually did better than I'd supposed.

The challenge is to reach a happy medium and have a moderate view of yourself. Not one of us is by any means insignificant, we all have our unique purpose to fulfill in life, and at the same time, not one of us is entitled to special respect, whatever rank you may belong to or aspire to. To think of ourselves properly, we must consider what makes someone "great."

Some people believe celebrities are great, but why? Mostly because they are paid well and are well-known by society, but how does that make them unique? It seems to me that most celebrities got where they are by means of either chance, friendly connections in their industry, or ruthlessly clawing their way to the top. None of these things makes them superior. Some celebrities, though not many, are truly admired for their kindness and compassion, using their high position and wealth to help others. You notice here that there is a difference between Greatness and Popularity.

The most revered and beloved people throughout history have been those who gave every last drop of their devotion to a noble cause or selflessly helping people. Think of Gandhi, Martin Luther King Jr., Robin Hood, Jesus of Nazareth, George Washington, Joan of Arc, and plenty more. Regardless of your opinions of such people, it is undeniable they are highly esteemed because of their unbreakable determination and service to others. If we aim to emulate their path and follow in their footsteps, we too cannot be selfish or even self-centered; we must be servants. We are to be servants, yes, but not slaves; free and sovereign, respectable, confident, and with purpose.

Mahatma Gandhi began his career being trained as a lawyer in London and subsequently moved to South Africa after a short period back in India. He supported the British in a war against the Boer minority despite his sympathizing with the Boers. He also supported the British Empire in World War I, believing India would gain independence after the war. When his hopes were disappointed, he began his satyagraha (nonviolent resistance) movement in earnest. This became his purpose in life, and he is well remembered for what he did thereafter. He simplified his life, living with less luxury than the average Indian peasant, which allowed him to focus on serving others.

Indeed, the key to being a servant to others and yet realizing our own significance is to find our personal purpose. Everybody has one, and there's no reason to even live at all without one. A purposeless person will inevitably be depressed and bored, perpetually sensing there is something missing in their lives. But even despite having a purpose, some become presumptuous, believing their wisdom to be of such great importance and scarcity that anybody lacking this wisdom is a fool. In order to avoid such a "high and mighty" attitude, we have to acknowledge our relative insignificance in the grand scheme of things. Yes, we each have a unique and important purpose, but if we fail to accomplish it, somebody else will; we are not likely divinely ordained prophets—so don't get "too big for your britches!"

But there's more to the story of self-confidence: the physical aspect. Now, unfortunately, this one is much more challenging because we can always change our minds, but only so much of our physical appearances can be changed. If we are not content and comfortable with our appearances, we will be sheepish and uncomfortable dealing with people. When I was younger, and my face mottled with blemishes, I was extremely embarrassed about my appearance and wished I could go off into the wilderness as a hermit and be seen by nobody. Eventually, I realized that if I had a confident way about how I carried myself, people seldom noticed my imperfections, or if they did, they didn't dwell on them too long.

Everybody has something to be thankful for in their looks. Now, I can't lie; some people are just plain ugly, or at least less showy than others. If you feel that you are in this category, ask yourself: "Am I being fair with myself or am I selling myself short." It may be that looks are really just not your strong suit, if so, consider focusing on just being a kindhearted person, having inner beauty (which is more important anyway), and likely, after getting to know you better, people will care less about how you look. But, why not do everything in your power to improve your looks? If you have some weight you'd like to lose, be determined to commit and live a more wholesome lifestyle to help you accomplish that goal. Living an active lifestyle, a diet low in sugar and carbohydrates, and being out in nature are sure to help. If you have a skin problem, say acne perhaps: go out in the sun, get a tan (which makes blemishes less noticeable), take cold showers (which close the pores and reduce inflammation), wash your face with baking soda, minimize your consumption of sugary processed foods, and exercise. It is a necessity that you find a way to content yourself with your appearance once you've done all you can to improve it, because your happiness will suffer otherwise.

Did your grandma ever tell you to "stand up straight and stop slouching"? If not, you've likely heard it somewhere else. Beyond the skeletal benefits of standing up straight, it also helps us feel at ease. Our body and mind are intricately connected: your mind affects the body and your body affects the mind. If you stand tall, relax your shoulders, puff out your chest, suck in your gut, raise your eyes high, and walk with a broad stride, you will feel more self-assured. Start good habits and they will change how you feel about yourself.

Once you are confident in your appearance and your purpose in life, you need to be confident in your ability to have intelligent conversations with people. If you believe that everybody is wiser than you, you will be shy, which is fine, but as I've found over the years, being uncomfortable around people is just plain unpleasant. It's much nicer to place no limits on yourself, be able to do anything, and be anywhere without feeling nervous.

Do you feel uptight around people? I know I sure did. I would get overpoweringly hot, start sweating, time would move unnaturally slow, and my eyes would even tear up. All that just from being in a crowd. Now I'm free of all those symptoms, except when I wear a woolen suit, I will get hot! Why? It takes work, but a good start is to realize this: what can people really do to you? The worst that could conceivably happen is for you to make an utter fool of yourself, and you might never see the person again anyway. If you do have to see them again, they'll understand, everybody makes mistakes. Nobody expects you to be perfect, except perhaps yourself. In which case, you need to get over perfectionism; do your best, whatever that may be, and ask for nothing more than that.

For a long time, I convinced myself that I enjoyed shyness, and was proud of it. If you want to be a "man of few words" then by all means do so, what you do say will be more highly respected when you say it and nobody will be able to criticize you for being a chatterbox. Nevertheless, I eventually realized that social timidity was simply fear, and nobody wants to be ruled by fear. If you want to be a hermit, be one! Just don't be afraid of what can't hurt you. Be quiet by choice, not by fear of making a fool of yourself.

For a long time when I used to be shy, people would always try and crack my shell, get me to talk. So they'd put me on the spot and pepper me with personal questions, which only made me feel more uncomfortable. But eventually, I realized that if I were to ask them a lot of questions (not being rude, just making conversation) to keep them on their toes, they'd oftentimes actually start looking around nervously and try to cut the conversation short. The reason for this unusual behavior is that dominant people like to dominate a conversation, and they enjoy speaking to children and shy people in general because they feel at ease with them and get the opportunity to dominate the conversation. It is seldom meant to be inconsiderate, certainly not malicious; they likely don't even realize they're doing it. But if you take advantage of a knowledge of how such people think, you can "give them their own medicine" and get the upper hand in what would usually be an awkward discussion. Understanding psychology at first makes one feel disgusted with people, believing everything they do is motivated by some subconscious primal impulse, but further knowledge permits one to have compassion for others, seeing as their intentions are pure. But we will discuss these subjects in more detail later on.

If you are downright horrified at the idea of having to ask outgoing, extroverted people questions, as was I, here are some suggestions to help. Try talking to yourself. Take a walk in the woods, the hills, the prairies, the beach, or some other isolated spot and have a full-blown conversation with yourself. If you are deliberating on a problem or coming to a decision on something, take both sides and debate the subject out loud. When you get accustomed to conversing naturally by yourself, it will also extend to real conversations with other people. To this day, I still go out in the backwoods and talk to the trees, sometimes speaking for them and other times letting the sound of the wind in their leaves do the answering. Strange perhaps to most people, I know, but beneficial for more than one reason. Another vital skill for mastering conversation is a robust vocabulary; so in order to build your word usage: read, read, and read; just like you're doing right now! Another thing to keep in mind is the physical side of things. If you feel good and have mental clarity, conversation will come easy, but if you feel sickly, bloated, and have brain fog, then you'd likely rather sit alone in the woods someplace. Remember, being a hermit is wonderful; I'd like to try it myself some time (at least till I start to miss people), but if social interaction is inescapable for you, then there's only one thing to do: learn to like it.

But what if you're already confident, perhaps too confident? If you come off to people as overbearing and domineering, they'll likely be put off by you. So how would you go about bringing your view of yourself back into balance? If you believe you are special, gifted, or skilled—you may well be right, but let's bring it into perspective. There will always be somebody who's better than you, no matter how skilled you may be. And even if you are exceptional and the best in the world at what you do, you can't be the best at everything! Everybody has their own strengths and weaknesses; learn to respect the strengths of others even if you don't understand them or would prefer your own skills. And not to scare you, but you do well to remember that your gifts could disappear in a blink of an eye, if some tragic accident befalls you and your skill could be snatched right out of your hands. Our skills are indeed gifts, so let's be grateful for them and likewise admire the gifts of others, neither disrespecting them nor envying them.

Another issue many folks encounter is the urge to compare themselves to others and judge themselves according to their observations. Each of us is an unfathomably complex, unmatchable, and singularly unique being with our own high purpose and beautiful, vast potential. Whether that potential is attained or not (as some people are born with disabilities or other encumbrances that hinder their ability to achieve their full potential), each of us is worthy of being assessed individually and not by somebody else's standard. If we do our very best and only that, and we constantly seek our continual betterment, we have nothing to be condemned for. Oftentimes, the standards that people set for themselves, they extend to all humanity, and if anybody doesn't measure up to their "right" level, that person or those people are deemed inferior. All cultures, societies, and even families and individuals are raised differently—it is not for us to judge.

At the same time, overconfidence in our abilities may lead to humiliation. I have noticed a few acquaintances who resolutely believed in their ability to accomplish something, namely throwing a football, but this overconfidence paralyzed and stunted their interest in practicing their skills. At the time, these friends of mine boasted of their athletic prowess, and so we proceeded to play a little game of football. The result was hilarious; upon flinging the ball, it turned over and over, not a bit of spin or arrow-like straightness to it, rather it veered off into the nearby woods. After such a spectacle, this individual attempted to excuse himself by a defense: his shoulder had been hurting, and he was off his game. And that may have been true, but he didn't see fit to mention that beforehand, which would have been more fitting than boasting. If perhaps this fellow, rather than talking up his skills, simply practiced his athletics, those who played with him might have been surprised and impressed, seeing fit to compliment him. It is better to be silent about our supposed skills, letting others compliment us instead, for if we ever cease to live up to our claims, we will be quite humbled.

Self-confidence also can have a cumulative effect on your performance in life. If you strongly believe in yourself, you are more likely to succeed in whatever your goal may be; and even if you fail, you learn from the mistake and try again with more experience. On the other hand, if from the very beginning you doubt your ability and have a negative attitude, your chances of success are lower, and failure will only reinforce that pessimistic attitude, so you will likely give up thereafter. This brings us to another subject: Optimism vs. Pessimism.

Some people believe it to be prudent to expect the worst and hope for the best so that if they fail, it will be no surprise, and if they succeed, it will be a pleasant and unexpected joy. The issue with that mentality is that it lessens your motivation to try and succeed because success seems a remote possibility not worth striving for. Instead, expect and strive for the best, and if such is not attained, then view the shortcoming as a lesson that will only enable you to do better next time. This idea is summed up in Mr. Thomas Edison's famous quote: "I never once failed. I just found 2,000 ways not to make a light bulb; I only needed to find one way to make it work." If we view every challenge not as a burden but as a lesson and gift to strengthen us and show us the way to our goals, then we will undoubtedly be quite content, at peace, and confident.

Our positive attitude about life should also apply to ourselves. As the saying goes: "we are our own worst critic." The average person finds it easy to excuse and forgive others for their little mistakes, but for themselves—it's quite another story. Such ones have compassion for others but very little left over for themselves. Don't be too hard on yourself; show yourself the same mercy you would show others.

At one of my old jobs, I worked at a family-run farm. My boss was an elderly grouch (but he was kind deep down though) and his daughter, let's call her Agatha, she was very self-deprecating. Her father excused no mistakes whatsoever and required everything to be done precisely his way, even if his workers found it easier, quicker, and more efficient to do it another way. Now Agatha, growing up in this environment, learned to be inordinately hard on herself so her father wouldn't. She prolonged this habit into adulthood. She certainly didn't treat people in the harsh way her father did, but she sure treated herself that way. If she forgot the slightest thing or made one trivial mistake, she would get worked up, calling herself a "[blank] idiot." This merciless attitude towards herself was undoubtedly unhealthy and resulted in constant disappointment and annoyance. Being from a more relaxed background myself, I was wholly unaccustomed to such an attitude about life. The people I meet in urbanized areas are like aggressive workhorses that push themselves and their companions bloody because they are in a rush all the time. Where I come from, people slow down and learn patience; they prioritize kindness and common sense over rigidity and rules. If more people could learn to live and think like country people, we'd have a happier and more confident world.

Your environment, even the weather can affect your attitude as well. Where I grew up, I'll tell you, no doubt about it; it was really hot! Blistering hot, in fact. Just step out the door, and you're already sweating bucketfuls, and after getting a few things done, you'd go inside and take about a half hour just to cool down and dry off. We tried to get our yard work done in the mornings and evenings when it was a little cooler, and the hard work like cutting, hauling, and burning dead trees we'd do come winter. Before I learned my lesson, I used to move, talk, and think a little faster and more intensely than I ought to have. I soon realized an important lesson for a hot climate: slow down or burn up. So I learned to talk slowly, move slowly and smoothly, and even think calmly and methodically. Getting impatient, frustrated, or agitated in any way, even a little bit, would cause my body to overheat. So I took the natural course of action: calm down. Ever since then, the heat bothers me less, and the cold bothers me more, but that's a story for another day. Not all of us had the good fortune to be born in the countryside, but we have got to learn those lessons to be at peace with the world and ourselves.

For the most part, we are our own worst critics, but sometimes, others can be. If we have to deal with verbally abusive and insulting people, and there is no reasonable way to escape associating with them, we need to learn a few things. First of all, remember that nobody's born a bully; something turns them mean. Perhaps they had an abusive parent or experienced trauma. Understanding this, we can hopefully find it in our hearts to pity them; really they're only hurting themselves—if they hurt you, it's because you let them. Oftentimes bullies simply feel insecure themselves, their own self-esteem is suffering. Deep down, they want to feel good about themselves, not feel worthless. So they may enviously attack you in order to get you to feel as bad as them. They may not think of it that way, likely they don't even know what they're doing. You need to develop a thick skin, just because they say something doesn't mean it's true. Try to learn to think logically, not emotionally; no, they haven't ruined your life, they're just trying to make it harder. The one who harms others harms himself, nobody else can harm us emotionally but ourselves. So don't let their taunts get to you; they are projecting their own problems onto you, just pity them— maybe even try to help them. When somebody is the hardest to love is when they need the most love. Try to kill them with kindness, and they likely won't be able to continue bothering you. If you give them some kindness (something they surely need whether they know it or not), not only will you help them but also yourself—it will boost your own confidence. You know, "what doesn't kill you makes you stronger."

Speaking of giving, another element of confidence is generosity. Giving to others helps us feel useful, gives us joy, and makes us feel like we have a purpose. How we give and who we give to is up to our personal preferences. Some like to donate to charity, others their religious organization, and still others like to give personally—to friends, family, even strangers. Have you ever noticed the glowing pleasure you feel when you give a gift to somebody? It's just plain good for us. Keep in mind, of course, that we would be nothing at all if we lived only for ourselves. We don't just want to improve our own lives, but also the lives of those around us. And it doesn't have to always be people, we can give to the earth as well. As a woodsman myself, there's nothing I like better than nurturing the land, helping it to be bountiful, help animals and plants to have an easier time. Not to get off topic, as this is no environmental book, but the next new housing development may seem to be an improvement to some people, but to the untamed denizens of that land it is a cataclysmic disaster that spells the end of the land that feeds them and made them in the first place.

A good part of the time, because of our busy lives, we have no time to rest and reflect in silence. When we are down or depressed, our mental vision has been clouded, making us unable to see things for how they are. No matter how troubled your life may be, there is ever so much to be grateful for. Instead of always lingering on the things that go wrong, why not list in our mind all the good things that happen each day.

Life itself is a wondrous miracle, with all its little details: the wind rustling in the treetops, the birds singing, a breath of fresh air, the smile of someone you love, even the way you move your fingers! What? Yes indeed, your body is an amazing thing, the unfathomable complexity of it, the dynamic movement we enjoy. Please try an experiment with me. Just look at the palm of your hand. Flex your fingers a couple times. Isn't it amazing to see how the tendons stretch at will by the unseen, unthought command of electrical signals in the brain?

Open your eyes each new day and see the world as if it were new, everything in it is completely unfamiliar. See the world as a child sees it, fascinated with the littlest, seemingly trivial things (in the eyes of an adult), exploring nature with fresh and twinkling eyes. Going out in the woods can help you see all this clearly. I do it all the time, the woods (or any wild place) soothes the soul. When in times of silence in the wilds, I'll ponder over such things. What was before a murky path will be laid open and bright before me. And if there's an unanswered question hanging yet in my mind, it will inevitably be answered soon as I step into the untamed land and out of mankind's chaotic creations. If you have no land on your property, perhaps find a peaceful park, or better yet, a graveyard. Believe me, traffic may constantly flow in and out of city parks, but it seldom is crowded in a graveyard, except for the dead—and it sure is quiet. Sorry to end on that note, but the sum of what you should remember from this chapter is this: we are what we make of ourselves. If we think small, we'll stay small, if we have grand ambitions, we will likely accomplish them. If we don't believe in ourselves, we will be weak and get nowhere, but if we do believe in ourselves: I can assure you, you will remain free and accomplish your purpose in happiness.

Chapter 2: Persuasive Techniques, First Impressions, and Body Language

What kind of first impression do you make? Do your eyes dart around, do you give a handshake like a wet dishrag, do you wear bedraggled clothes or a hoodie, slouch over and walk like somebody screwed your joints together a little bit loose? Hopefully not! Why? Because, by golly, that would make a terrible first impression. Your prospective employer, friend, or otherwise would likely take you for a hoodlum. Many people nowadays are never taught how to give a good first impression. But it's necessary to do so because it will shape their whole perception of you for a long time and can make or break your plans. As such, let's go over some important points to keep in mind.

Handshake. If you go up to somebody and give them a handshake like you've got no bones in your hand, they'll take you for an unreliable person. To give a good handshake, always lean on the side of too tight rather than too loose. Try and match or slightly exceed the grip of the other person. It should be firm, but don't treat their hand like a squeeze ball for stress. Remember, it's no contest. If you want to have a thumb war or arm wrestle, do it on your own time. Don't try and see who can squeeze the hardest; and if the person is elderly, please don't break their hand! Everything in moderation.

Posture. Don't slouch; you'll seem shifty and disrespectful. Stand up straight like a pine tree and walk with a broad, robust stride. You can by all means, keep your hand in your pocket, but don't put the hand all the way in, and definitely don't put both in. Remember, perception, perception, perception. It might sound silly, it might be unreasonable, and you might not like it, but it's just the way it is. Use it to your advantage.

Eye contact. If you look at the ground and dart your eyes around, you'll seem nervous, insincere, and untrustworthy. You may well be nervous, but you don't need to proclaim to everybody! Look them straight in the eye and don't look away, let them look away. In casual conversation, there's nothing wrong with looking around as you talk, but formal discussion demands strict eye contact. If they choose to look away, let them, just don't you do it. Steady eye contact denotes integrity, dignity, and reliability to people. You certainly want to reflect those virtues.

Dress. A rule I've heard is: in a job interview, dress one level above what you'd generally wear at the job. If you're being interviewed to be a farm worker, you don't need to wear a three-piece suit, in fact, to do so would invite too much attention and possibly ridicule. For example, if you're being interviewed for a carpentry job, nice jeans and a button-down shirt, perhaps even corduroy pants, would do fine. You likely will wear worn and faded work pants while working, but you want to put your best foot forward.

Speech. Colloquial language, if not vulgar, is probably fine. The main rule of thumb is to try and reciprocate the language of the person you talk to. If they are formal, you act formal; if they are laid back, you should be relaxed, too. Be all things to all people. Even if you are used to cursing, it may not offend you, but you can safely assume that it will bother others. Of course, there's nothing inherently wrong with particular verbal sounds. If I moved to Ethiopia and learned to speak Amharic and there was some word in that language that sounded exactly like an English curse word, I wouldn't refrain from saying it, it wouldn't bother me at all. Why? Vulgarity is all about the connotation, or feeling that the word conveys; in other words, the power we give the word. Many people sprinkle curse words into every other word they speak.

They curse when they're happy, they curse when they're sad, they curse when they're laughing, and they curse when they're mad. Curse words are just a crutch that people lean on for lack of meaningful vocabulary. The curse word may mean nothing to you, but it may be shocking to somebody else. Do be careful to bridle your tongue.

Persuasive techniques are a useful tool that helps convince people of your viewpoint. It is good in an argumentative debate, when pleading your case for forgiveness, and even making employers interested in hiring you. You have to stand out from the crowd; you have to be a needle in the haystack. If you don't distinguish yourself by your principled virtues and impressive competence, you rely merely on chance that you may be chosen for a job, friendship, courtship, etc. There are several persuasive techniques you can use and some to avoid; we'll go over them one by one.

Let's start with the three most general and commonly used ones. First is Pathos. Pathos is useful and has its proper place, but it is unfortunately relied upon too heavily these days. It is an appeal to emotion, sentiment, and feelings. Its goal is to stir up strong feelings in somebody's heart in order to steer their thinking in your desired direction. Here's a common example: have you ever seen those ASPCA animal rights commercials? If so, you'll recall the sad music, the unusually dirty and deformed dogs, and the pleading voice asking for your donation. Now it's certainly a worthy cause, but the argument is based on your feelings, not reason. It hopes you will be moved with pity and sadness for these poor animals and will conclude the best course of action is to donate to the ASPCA. Another example of this is pharmaceutical commercials. These, you will notice, show beautiful weather and play upbeat music, portraying healthy-looking people participating in jolly, enjoyable activities. The intention is to capture your attention and direct it to all the pleasant scenes they portray; and even more important, to distract your attention from the drug's ingredients and the remarkably fast-paced voice outlining all the disturbing side-effects. Sound familiar? Unfortunately, most big news outlets rely on emotional bluster to get the point across, and it works. If you are trying to influence dull-witted or tired people to your side, this is undoubtedly by far the best technique. Such a strategy will not appeal, though, to logical people too well, which brings us to the next point.

Logos. Logos is an appeal to logic or reason. It avoids emotionality and primarily focuses on cause-and-effect scenarios that attempt to argue that a certain course of action is the most prudent. An example of this is gold buying commercials. You might not remember such commercials, they were more common in the past. But the general idea is that the value of the dollar (fiat currency) is going down, inflation is going up, and an economic downturn seems just around the corner. As gold does not lose value, rather, has been gaining value, it is a wise investment to purchase for an uncertain future. This technique is reasonable and admirable, but the only problem with it is that many people simply don't like to think, they like to be spoon-fed thoughts from others, and such reasoning may go over their heads, in which case you might try and simplify the idea to get the point across. Methodically explain the reasoning step by step, asking questions along the way—this will definitely help them understand most of the time.

The third technique is Ethos. Ethos is an appeal to principle, ethics, and morality. Of course, right off the bat you can discern that such rhetoric would not work on unprincipled and immoral people, but thank goodness, most people do not completely fall into that category. Much political and almost all religious rhetoric involves Ethos, calling on people's morality to guide their path of decision-making.

Another related principle is the subject of honor. Honor is usually framed within an official or unofficial code of honor, which sets the standard for respectable behavior. The early colonial United States had a very strong culture of honor which dictated many activities, historical and even present-day. Some sections of the United States and the world in general still have this culture of honor, especially in traditional, religious, and rural communities. All men and women of honor are careful to avoid giving direct counsel to someone, usually speaking very generally in the third person—seldom addressing the recipient directly. Also, insulting someone even in a small way, is strongly avoided unless somebody wants to end up in a verbal or physical altercation.

In the old days, even a mild insult quite often became a duel that resulted in the death of one man or the other. Thankfully, few of us ever have to fear this outcome, but it is nevertheless a wise course of action to craft your words carefully if you want to appeal to people. Honor also incentivizes people to maintain a highly respected reputation in their community. In some cases, this can lead to insincere people becoming obsessed with appearances, hiding their true darker nature from others, but that is a clear misuse of honor. Truly honorable people stand up for what they believe in, fight for it tooth and nail to their last breath, and remain impeccably aligned with their principles no matter what difficulties it may bring them—regardless of convenience. Wherever you come from, whatever culture, whatever background: are not these certainly high-minded ideals we can all aspire to?

In addition, when we are trying to convince people of our view, we need to keep in mind some argumentative fallacies we do best to avoid. Now, do remember that if your argument does contain a fallacy, fallacy does not mean "inherently false." And it certainly wouldn't falsify your whole argument—it only means a weakness that could be criticized by opponents. With that in mind, let us proceed.

Bandwagon. The bandwagon fallacy is a psychological technique people use to make you feel left out. It implies: "Everybody is doing something, so you should do it too, don't get left behind!" Children use this habitually: "Hey Bo, how about we get you a smoke?" Says Bo, "Nah, Frank, I don't know about that. My ma got lung cancer smoking." Says Frank, "Oh come on, everybody's doing it!" Poor Bo. What significance is in the number of people doing a thing, and why it matters, I don't have the slightest idea. The true standard by which we should make decisions is logic and reason, even if we're the only ones doing it, if we believe it's the right thing to do, do it.

Next up is the Strawman or red herring. In the middle of a discussion, sometimes an individual with a disadvantage in the argument will toss out a red herring. A red herring or strawman fallacy is when someone inserts a random comment into a conversation in order to distract attention from the subject at hand. An example: John is the owner of a logging company, and he is interviewing a possible new employee. John says to his interviewee, "So Jim, do you got some experience in wood cutting?" Says Jim, "I love burning wood, my house has a nice wood stove, and it keeps us warm all winter." John responds, "Um, that's nice, Jim. Do you got any wood-cutting experience, though?" Jim's random interjection did not at all answer John's question. He only said it because he didn't want to answer the question.

Politicians especially can have the bad habit of refusing to answer questions and instead babbling on about nonsense that has nothing to do with what was being talked about. Another mistake politicians can make that you should never pick up is driveling. They are skilled at using many words to say practically nothing at all. If you have a complex idea to articulate, you may by all means, use fancy technical jargon, but never do it just to sound smart because a truly intelligent person will notice and take you for an idiot. If you are a fool, don't try and hide it, it only makes things worse. A fool is acceptable, a lying fool is not.

Another fallacy, the slippery slope. The slippery slope fallacy is when someone makes an unsupported assumption that if things continue as they are, they will inevitably lead to something unexpected. For example, "If loggers keep cutting down the Amazon Rainforest like this, it'll be gone in 20 years!" This was a statement many "experts" were making a few decades back. Clearly though, the Amazon is still intact, though as civilization continues making inroads into the forest, it has begun to be fragmented. The truth is that most slippery slope arguments actually have some validity, but you cannot just assume, you must have evidence for the result you believe will happen.

Circular Reasoning. This fallacy is another way people can sound smart as long as no one listens too carefully. It is when somebody attempts to explain their point but simply repeats the sentiment in different words. For instance, "I am a pretty good speaker because I express what I want to say very well." It might sound fine at first glance, but you notice the latter part of that sentence essentially means: "I am a good speaker." So in reality, what I am saying is this: "I am a good speaker because I am a good speaker." See how you think I was going to say something new there, but then I just repeated myself? It's like a circle, and thus the name—

circular reasoning. Clearly, repeating what you just said is not a strong or convincing argument.

Next, the No True Scotsman fallacy. Let's head right into the example with this one. Hannah says, "No man says the word 'fabulous.'" Mary responds, "Johnny says 'fabulous' all the time!" Hannah's retort: "Johnny must not be a real man then." Do you get the point? Good, then let's move on.

The Texas Sharpshooter fallacy is best described by the origin of the name. A Texan wanted to prove he was a real good shot with his squirrel rifle, so he fired a few bullets into a wall. Afterwards, he drew a target on the wall—with his bullet-holes right in the middle of the bullseye! Scientists and researchers can be tempted to cherry pick data to support their hypothesis despite the fact that the whole rest of the data disagrees with the hypothesis. A practical example of this: Scientist Sam says: "I believe more trees are dying than average because we've been getting more rain. I tested recently-killed trees and found that they had more moisture around their soil than living trees. That proves it." His colleague says, "Well Sam, there's lots of reasons that might be. Anyhow, we had a drought this year." Our Sam had his hypothesis, but failed to address all the data.

Now that we've gone over argumentative logic, let's dive into body language. Body language is a universal form of communication, though it does vary widely from species to species. Non-human animals use body language much more extensively than humans, though such animals still usually make use of vocal language. Think of birds singing, dolphins clicking, and so forth. Humans, on the other hand, are not as fluent in body language, often even oblivious to it.

An example of a man who defied that pattern was Monty Roberts; Monty Roberts grew up in a rodeo family and often participated in horse training, but from an early age, he seemed to disagree with the traditional horse training methods, seeing them as cruel and breaking the spirit of a horse. When he had the opportunity, he traveled from his home in the Salinas Valley of California to the High Desert of Nevada. There, he watched the movements of wild mustangs, but he noticed something that most people did not— their body language.

He was completely colorblind, seeing only black and white, and for that reason, he was more sensitive to movement. He eventually learned the consistent body language of all horses, wild or tame, which he calls Equus, and he uses it to his advantage in gently training horses. What may seem to be an impediment, that is, complete color blindness (seeing in black and white only), ended up being an advantage to Mr. Roberts, letting him see the world differently. Though he may have discovered this special method of horse training, which he calls "Join-Up," many other horsemen around the world use it as well. In fact, it became so popular in the equestrian world that the late Queen Elizabeth II of England invited him to show his method to her. In the same way, if we are careful to observe the body language and subtle movements of the people around us, we will better understand them and appeal to them. It can be simple enough by context and observation to discern the internal feelings of others; doing so will help us be more empathetic.

The most obvious and apparent form of body language is facial expression. In the Western World at least, politeness dictates we ought to look people in the eye, and therefore we notice facial expressions better than anything else. Despite this, focusing on only one detail can blind us to what else may be going on, so we're better off paying attention to a variety of signs.

Happiness and excitement can be discerned by observing the general energy with which they walk: that is, broad and quick strides. Also, lips will be upturned in a grin, the muscles on the cheek will be strained upwards and somewhat wrinkled, their eyes will be likely to be turned upwards as they walk, their eyes will squint and wrinkle at the corners, and the person's voice will likely be louder, faster, and higher pitched. Hopefully, this will be the expression you see most often!

Sadness is quite the opposite of happiness, both in subjective sensation and appearance. Their voice will be low, slow, and quiet; their face will droop with eyes slightly closed and looking downwards, cheeks relaxed, and lips turned down in a frown. Along with all that, movement will be slowed and dragging.

Anger is similar to sadness but much more intense. There will likely be a strong frown and furrowed eyebrows that extend the wrinkle into the forehead. Unlike the slow and suppressed movement of sadness, the movement will be fast, the voice loud and low, and the stare intense. Yelling, wild gestures, and violence can go hand in hand with unbridled wrath.

Focus is often indicated when a person locks their eyes on one thing, scrunching their eyebrows together and almost frowning. They will have a strong determination to get the job done and may become more impatient or irritable if anybody hinders their work. Focus can be manic, done in desperation, and associated with anger and stress. On the other hand, focus can be enjoyable and indicate the person has a purpose and enjoys participating in the activity they're engaged in. Another sign of focus can be observed while conversing with somebody, if they look upwards and move their eyes back and forth, this denotes they are trying to recall something (and may possibly be ignoring what you're saying to them). A lack of focus could take many forms. The person's eyes may drop, and their posture may look lethargic. Another common thing to see is when somebody has wide eyes looking out into space, which denotes a lack of enthusiasm and profound disinterest, shock, or dissatisfaction with whatever is going on. Stress is very similar to focus in appearance (albeit in a negative, manic form of focus) and may also involve nervous mannerisms like wringing the hands, twirling the hair, or running the hands through the hair on either side of the head and pressing into the temples.

Confidence is similar to happiness in most respects, and a truly happy person will usually be confident, so the two go hand in hand. They will make eye contact, speak forcefully and assertively, not doubtful of their abilities.

Fear is quite easy to notice because a person's natural inhibitions fly away in the face of terror. They may scream, cower, raise their cheeks without squinting the eyes (same as one would do when in pain), their lips could be clasped tightly shut, their posture is rigid, goosebumps may form, and gasping is quite likely.

The body language of dishonesty is often attempted to be hidden by the lier, but can be done sloppily, and thus a keen-eyed person can spot it. The person may lower their eyes, dart their eyes around, act shifty and fidgety, along with a very rigid posture. Another sign of lying is overdoing it, trying so hard to act truthfully that it becomes evident that the person is trying to hide something. Despite the fact that these may be common signs of dishonesty, there are plenty of other reasons why one may act this way. As such, it is always a good idea to give people the benefit of the doubt; if you can assume good or assume bad, then assume good. Try to see the best in people, and don't be suspicious or jealous. Don't let yourself be led along, but don't be overly cautious either. And when you associate yourself with people, try to take note of their honesty or lack thereof; you would never want to be stuck with an untrustworthy friend, or worse yet, an untrustworthy spouse. Do not choose your friends for superficial reasons because you may well regret it later.

Another type of body language, the type that is most often mentioned, is the cues that can occur between the opposite sex during courtship. A question that many young people ask during such a time is: "Does [so-and-so] like me?" Well, here are some pointers that could help answer that question.

A flirtatious pose is obvious, there is no mistaking it, and as such there is no reason for me to describe it—it varies greatly from person to person. Therefore what I will describe are the more subtle cues, those that can be mistaken. Sometimes, neither person may even realize they are exhibiting these signals. You should be aware of them so that you can avoid doing them if you don't want to, or that you can notice them in others as you interact. Most important of all to keep in mind is that these are not sure signs by any means. Many of these mannerisms are simply common in kindhearted people, but if you notice them in somebody that only exhibits them towards you—that would be the true sign that they have a deeper care for you.

If you mention to this person a little thing in passing, something you wouldn't expect them to remember, and they later repeat it to you or ask you a question about it, that shows the person is paying very close attention to what you say and do—indicating either that the person is very observant and possesses a good memory or that the person cares very much about you and made sure to take a mental note of what you said.

Attraction. Do they linger around you all the time and work with you if at all possible? Or they may even choose to avoid you in order not to bother you too much, in which case you may not notice. They may also take every opportunity, even when it is inconvenient for them, to talk with you, to check on how you're doing, and contact you through texting or calling you. This indicates that the person is frequently thinking about you and has a strong desire to be with you all the time.

Posture. The person will smile, stand straight up, with arms not crossed, hands either in the pockets, on the hips, or hanging at the sides. Their feet will face you directly, not turned at all to the side. They may brush against you frequently or touch your arm or shoulder. They will keep prolonged eye contact with you the whole time you are talking together, not turning away very often. Blushing is also a common indication of attraction. Blushing is caused by the release of various chemicals throughout the body that makes one feel excited, redden the skin, raise heartbeat and body temperature, and cause sweating thereby. Now, a habit of working together always indicates two people like each other, but it may not necessarily mean they love you in a special way.

Voice. Nervous stuttering, awkward speech, constantly asking questions, and a lot of laughing without anything funny happening can be a clue of attraction in some less confident people. The male will soften his voice, making it slightly more high-pitched, whereas the female will deepen her voice. This universal tendency is not done in an exaggerated way, just enough to equalize the two different voices so that they synchronize in pitch, speed, rhythm. It's like a beautiful song where the desire is to reach harmony by compromising together. This is also something empathic people will frequently do with everyone, which is something we will discuss later.

Mimicry. Somebody that wants to appeal to you will subconsciously mimic your behavior, your accent, your expressions, your mannerisms, your stance, and your facial expressions. A more silly and poor attempt at this is when somebody pretends to like everything you like. Of course, if the two of you really have that much in common, all the better. But pretenses are never a good idea to maintain. Pretenses are like a mask, as long as it is realistic and believable, it goes fine, but as soon as the mask is taken off, the truth is revealed.

As aforementioned, please remember that all these subtle cues are signs of friendship, attraction, and care. Caring people will naturally do most of these things to everyone they meet, and not at all in a romantic way. But whether that care is friendly or romantic is often very difficult to tell. The only surefire way to know for certain is if they tell you or you ask them point-blank.

Chapter 3: Empathy

First of all, let's see what's the difference between empathy and sympathy. Sympathy is essentially pitying a person and wishing them well. For example, "Aw, Jarmy got rheumatism, poor soul! I hope the herbalist can help him." Sympathy is simply taking action to show your concern for the plight of another—empathy goes much deeper. Empathy is truly feeling what they're feeling, walking in their shoes. It denotes a connection so deep as to allow an exchange of emotions between two people. Sympathy is to "feel bad for" someone, whereas empathy is to "feel with" someone. Do you see the distinction here?

Now empathy is certainly a noble virtue of the highest degree, something which all people ought to pursue, but it does have its drawbacks. Anything in too great or too little in quantity can be out of balance; as the saying goes, "Everything in moderation." If we have extreme empathy for every unfortunate person we meet and every unpleasant situation we hear of, we will certainly be miserable. In the past, most people only knew of the news that went on in their own little neck of the woods, and every once in a while, they'd hear of something going on in a big city nearby. Nowadays, we have the world at our fingertips, quite literally. We have access to all the news from the whole world; and in a world such as this, there seems to be far more bad news than good. Nobody can take the whole world on their shoulders! Let us each bear our own burdens, and also help with the burdens of those near us, but we are incapable of bearing the whole world's troubles all by ourselves. Some people are naturally empathetic, they intuitively see the pain of those around them, and it hurts them. By all means, let's do all in our power to help others, but we cannot be brought down by the various evils that plague the world. We do best to be strong, rocky islands that laugh at the most vicious tempest as it violently dashes into the island's rocks, and yet no flood can wash it away. Nonetheless, too much empathy is a rare problem; more often is too little empathy the issue.

Now, if we are already empathic, good, but if not, how do we cultivate empathy in ourselves? One of the foremost reasons we might fail to show empathy is that we have trouble understanding the feelings of others. This could make people feel that you are uncompassionate, unfeeling, and harsh. A simple way to remedy this would be to imagine yourself in their situation, their background, their strengths and weaknesses. When I have found myself being inconsiderate to others, I will put myself in their shoes, and immediately my mistake is made clear. Remember that everybody has a different way of thinking, which could influence how they experience life. If you are tough as nails, a friend that is traumatized by what seems to you a trivial thing, could put a wedge between you and your friend. Consider instead how they think. Do you give people coffee the way they like it or the way you like it? The very basis of all religion and morality is to "do to others only what you would want them to do to you." If the Golden Rule is universally followed, there is little room for error.

But empathy should go beyond a mere feeling—it should lead to action. When a loved one is hurting, we can comfort them. When a friend, acquaintance, or even a stranger needs something, we do everything in our power to give it to them. Sympathy is just consoling somebody: "I'm so sorry, Jim. You have my sincerest condolences. If there's anything you need, just tell me." It's all good and well to wish someone well, but you know our poor fictional Jim here doesn't want to be a bother, he likely won't ask his friend even if he does need something. We have to take the initiative and give them something they'd like. We don't need to be rich to give a gift; a gift can be our time, our love, a visit, a conversation, some help in the house or on the land. Anything really can be a gift, but the gifts we give depend on a few things, which we will discuss next.

Each of us has different ways we prefer to show love and receive love. If we don't understand how other people feel about love, we may seem cold and uncaring. Here are a few ways people show love; most people prefer one of the following or a combination of a few.

Touch. Many sensitive and emotional people show love by touch, the most obvious way. They like to hug, kiss, touch, touch, and touch. To other similar people, these expressions of care are perfectly fine, but to others, it can be quite annoying and embarrassing. Sometimes, more logical people will perceive "touchy-feely" love as shallow and sappy, but this is not necessarily always the case. Some people are truly sincere in their physical love. As long as the love goes deeper than touch, it is fine. But our love should be based on more than words and hugs, it should be proven by how we treat others. I knew a family very well once who were very outwardly loving, very "touchy-feely," but they were not sincerely so. The father in the family was very demanding, particular, and judgemental; the mother was very negative, dishonest, manipulative, and loved to complain and bemoan her lot in life. In this case, hugs and kisses didn't really mean true and genuine love.

Words. Others enjoy being told they are loved and given gifts. They live off of encouragement and attention; if they don't receive it, they'll believe you don't love them. They'll expect you to give them your complete attention and all the spare time you've got. If you seem distracted when you are spending time with loved ones, if you don't give direct and continuous eye contact, if you leave even for a moment to take care of some business or something for work, they will automatically interpret this as you wanting to get away from them. I knew a lady who said that her father always said he loved her till one night when she was seven years old or so. He never said it again, and she believed that she had disappointed him somehow. She never felt loved, but rather that she was a responsibility that her father took seriously. We wouldn't want our loved ones to feel that way about us. Even if actions mean more to us than words, we need to take into consideration that not all people feel that way. It may seem silly to us, but can't we humor them and just say: "I love you?" It can be very hard to start doing something we're not used to, and there may be various reasons why this may be too much for some people—for now, at least.

Some folks, usually country women, show love through food. They do a good bit of cooking and are really good at it. Their recipes are passed down for many generations and are well-revered by the family. In some more traditional, old-fashioned, backwoods homesteads, the man will go out hunting, fishing, tending the herd of wild hogs, and tending the cornfield. The woman will take care of the garden and orchards, draw water, and do the cooking. That's how they show love—a literal labor of love. This is still more or less the way things are done in many backcountry households in the US and around the world. Some people live more primitive than that, and others live more modern, but the point is: in a self-sufficient clan, work is love, for work is how everybody stays on the right side of the dirt, if you know what I mean (nobody wants to be six foot under—in a casket, I mean).

The last group we have here are those who expect action from someone who loves them. To people like this, words mean nothing, words can be an act. Gifts, attention, and quality time mean nothing because anybody can pay a little money and give a little time to get something they want out of somebody else. And then, such people believe, when people get tired of you, they'll cast you aside. What really means something to them is the little things. Do you compromise with them, do you help them, do you seem to genuinely enjoy their company? Essentially, do you care about them for who they are, even when you ask nothing from them? That is what they're looking for, all the outward forms of love just seem to shield reality. When you help people and care about them out of the goodness of your heart, when you have nothing to gain—that is what is trustworthy. Such people are usually critical thinkers, stoic, calculating, and based on reason and logic, and personal experience. My grandfather was one such man. He never talked about love, seldom hugged or touched, but he'd show it by the concern he had for others and the way he'd help people at his own expense. I greatly admire the man and aim to follow in his footsteps in that regard, yet at the same time, be capable of showing love in different ways if that's what other people want.

Love should never be an act, a mask that you take on and off at will. It must be genuine and earnest; otherwise, people will see right through it. And as I said before: give people their coffee the way they want it, not the way you want it. Give people love how they like it, not how you like it. Yes, it can be a challenge, it definitely is for me, but it's necessary in order to be a happy and well-loved person.

Our goal is never to force people to do what we want, to manipulate them, to control them. Certainly not. Our goal is to just be a caring person; this will naturally result in winning friends and influencing them for the better. And I can tell you from experience, it really works. I truly do not mean to brag about what I'm about to say; I'm going to tell you this story only as an example so as to help you see the results of common kindness. In school, I showed myself to be a patient, gentle, quiet, confident, helpful, and happy person. When somebody looked like they were having trouble with something, I helped them and was gentle and compassionate all the time. But I wasn't always that way though; I used to be an occasionally immature, inconsiderate, rude, disrespectful, hot-tempered fellow. But I noticed that the people I most enjoyed being around were always mild and meek, so it was only right I should be such a person as well. It is not really all that complicated, none of us were born mean. Our subconscious trauma and unpleasant experiences lead us to bad habits of dealing with people, which become ingrained over time. If you've been unkind or not quite the mildest of people, you might think it would be fake if you started to be nice now. You might think it's too late, but I guarantee you, if you start being kind now, it'll feel natural. The people around you might be surprised, but I'm sure they'll be pleased, too. If you start being kind hearted now, you'll help yourself, not just your loved ones, friends, and acquaintances. If you are impatient and short-fused, consider this: if you made a mistake little or big, wouldn't you want to be treated with mercy and swiftly forgiven? Well then, give others the same.

How can we uproot deeply rooted and thoroughly ingrained habits from our personality? And more than that, how do we go beyond just "acting" kind to really "being" kind? How do we make loving kindness our very identity, so that our very presence is pleasant and soothing to all those around us? Sounds like a big thing to accomplish, but really, unkindness is unnatural, not kindness, so all of us have it deep inside somewhere.

Baruch Spinoza, the philosopher of philosophers, a 1600s Dutchman of Portuguese Jewish origin, determined how to overcome our baser impulses. He believed that a passive or subconscious impulse/emotion (an urge which we know we have, but do not want it, nor know why we have it) can be turned into an active/conscious emotion (a feeling we choose and are aware of) if we come to understand the reasons behind the subconscious emotion. Basically, he said that we could gain control over our habits and actions if we know the reason why we have them—the root cause.

As a personal example: when I was a young boy, I was much taller than my fellows, and I liked it. I loved being tall, and at the rate I was growing, the doctors projected me to grow to about 6'6". I was just an early bloomer, though, and soon stopped short. I hoped I would get another growth spurt, though. Shortly thereafter, my younger brother shot up past me and was soon over 6 foot, and I ended up being a good 8 inches shorter.

Now I was looking up at my "little" brother, and everybody that knew us pointed it out constantly, every time we saw people they'd mention how my brother had outgrown me. Now, this really did bother me profoundly. But later, I began to understand that height doesn't decide your athletics, character, ability, or much else. I had been thinking of height as a competition, something that would give me an advantage. I realized that I had certain perceptions of what a "real man" should be. I couldn't imagine my future wife being taller than me, it mortified me at just the thought!

It was a real hangup for me, I was very wrapped up in height, but when I realized that my obsession with height was silly, didn't matter, and was unfounded, I stopped caring whether or not my brother was taller than me or whether women were taller than me. I even stopped caring when people that knew us pointed it out. I started to laugh about it.

So when this happened, I was walking in the woods in the crisp, cool, vibrant Fall time, and I was pondering over all these things. Surprisingly, the very moment I realized this, all my perturbations regarding my height instantly disappeared, and I actually began to appreciate my height. All the various benefits of being shorter dawned on me right then. I felt content immediately. A subconscious imbalance that had been limiting me, something I never realized was affecting me so much— disappeared in a blink of an eye just because I realized why I felt that way. That can happen to you, too. You'll never know how much the depths of your mind can affect your life, for better or worse, unless you take the time to do what I did. Get yourself out of whatever building you are currently in, get out in mother nature (forgive me if you already are outside), and reflect on your life. Being constantly distracted and entertained is a good way to interfere with your clarity of mind. Take a break from doing all the time, and start just being.

That brings us to the subject of mindfulness and meditation. Mindfulness sounds simple but can be difficult. It is living in the present moment, thinking of only one thing at a time, not letting your mind dart off to other things. When you're walking, think only of the movements of your body and your surroundings. When you are washing your hands, think only of that. When you are thinking or pondering, perhaps planning for the future (nobody expects you to never think ahead at all), then do nothing else and focus on thinking. Imagine your mind as going to war. When you think of many different things, you are sending parts of your military force off in different places, spreading them out, dividing them. An army is never as strong when it is divided. We want our minds to be like a focused, unbreakable, invincible force to be reckoned with, one that marches altogether. Unite the thoughts within your mind to accomplish enthusiastically whatever you may be doing. So you are reading now, then think only of reading and read with all your might. You may eat a meal hereafter, then don't let yourself eat for comfort, don't overeat, focus on that one activity, and you will feel when your body is content. If you are running, think of nothing else, run with all you might. That is mindfulness, and you really cannot be stressed out when you are completely mindful. Your mind will never grow weary, get frazzled or frayed, no, it will be at peace and in focus.

Meditation is done in many ways. Some people meditate on a sacred text such as the Bible or some other sacred book, others meditate on their breath, others meditate while looking at a light, some meditate on some sound or mantra, others meditate on visualizing some image or scenario, some meditate on their heartbeat, and it goes on and on and on. People tend to believe that their form of meditation is the only true form, but is that really true? All the forms of meditation I listed above have a commonality: a fastener. What is a fastener? If you were in a fishing boat and you wanted to stay in one spot for a long time, what would you do? You'd cast down the anchor, and that would fasten you to one place until you were ready to raise the anchor. If you were tanning an animal hide and you needed to hold the skin in place in order to scrape the fat off, you would tie it in place around a frame. If you're camping and you set up a tent, you'd drive tent pins into the ground. If you want to keep wood in place, you nail it together. In the same way, if you want to direct your mind toward one thing only, in complete focus, you need a fastener, you need to hold your mind in place, so it doesn't drift away. You need to tie it to one spot. In meditation, a fastener is something very simple that you focus on in order to empty your mind of everything unimportant. People have different goals with meditation, some more or less ambitious than others. Some people say they are emptying their minds of everything, but in meditation, that is almost never the case. The focus accomplished in meditation is always done by means of some fastener to hold you in place, something for you to figuratively hold onto; so meditation is essentially emptying your mind of everything but one thing, and that gives you the ability to focus like a laser beam on that one thing in order to have a more powerful mind capable of doing extraordinary things.

If you are unaccustomed to meditation, I'll recommend one way to you. The eyes actually have influence over your mind; when you are thinking intensely, your eyes will automatically dart around even with your eyes shut. You know Rapid-Eye-Movement Sleep (REM sleep)? That is a period of sleep in the latter part of the night in which dreams are most intense; it received its name because of the rapid darting around the eyes at this time. So here's the simple meditation method: while awake, hold your eyes at one particular point in the distance and un-focus them so that your vision looks blurry. Hold your eyes in that position for as long as you'd like, and you will be unable to think of anything. The focus of controlling your eyes and the fact that you will be purposefully taking advantage of their physiology will ensure that your mind is unable to dart around like it usually does. This is a good start.

But some might wonder: what do meditation and mindfulness have to do with empathy? A valid question, by all means because many people think of meditation as being merely a self-improvement strategy, but it is so much more than that. Meditation and mindfulness give you the ability to live in the present moment, which allows you to respond to your environment in a wiser way. Being mindful does not mean that your mind is "full," no, on the contrary, it means that your mind is altogether empty. Usually, while we drive, do house work, work in the fields, and any other activity we may think of as drudgery, we operate mindlessly, relying on muscle memory and previous experience to guide our actions as we let our minds drift off onto other subjects (as a side note: for anybody who wants an example of the subconscious mind at work, consider how you can drive for a while, get to your destination, and not even remember anything about the trip: your subconscious mind was at work).

Rather than letting our minds dart around while we vacantly do something without focusing on it, we'd do better to instead not to think at all. Consciously perform any task, and the little joys of life will return to you. If you walk past the same view every day and you no longer pay attention to it, focus instead on each step you take and the path ahead of you; you will see the beauty of it again. In the same way, we will automatically see how to treat others lovingly when we are living consciously in the moment. We will say to ourselves: "How could I have said that?" or, "How could I have thought that was acceptable before?" And we will have the opportunity to correct our course, to get back on the right path. Life is not the past, life is not the future, life is the present. Not the present year, not the present month, not the present day, but the very second or millisecond you are currently in. Yes, we must more or less consider the future to allow it to guide our present actions, and we do the same with the past, though we should never be limited by either. Live now like you'd want the future to be. Life is not a destination, it's a journey. If you can't enjoy the journey, then there's no purpose to life before you reach your goal, or even after you reach your goal! Purpose can only be found in the present. Don't wait for the perfect time to do something, that time may never come. Do not be shortsighted and brash, but neither be so methodical and lumbering and ponderous that you can never get anything done.

If you live in the present, you will still make use of logic and reason, but deep feelings and intuition will be your foremost guide. When you live in the present, you will notice things you never did before, see the world with fresh eyes, let go of your preconceptions, and feel for people, places, and creatures that never crossed your mind before. Living in the present is the key to all sorts of things because it gives you a clear mind, which enables you to see things as they really are, see your purpose, and act accordingly. I am still struggling to implement this myself, I am not perfect. It is a challenge in the modern world to get rid of distractions enough to focus on only one thing at a time. Some jobs and activities require multitasking, which is a great enemy of mindfulness. In order to see how to reduce distractions in our lives in a practical manner and see some ways of showing empathy, we will now discuss how to live a more simple, peaceful life.

We now have a good start for showing empathy for people, but what about the earth, our own native land and the creatures in it? Is not our compassion also due and appropriate for nature? In order to live compassionately towards nature, we may consider seeing how we could simplify our lives. We don't all need to be hunter-gatherers in the wilderness or even farmers, but we can minimize the harm we bring nature and maximize the benefit to it. Many environmentalists consider humans as a parasite upon the earth; this view I cannot agree with. Humans actually have the potential to be an important contributor to the balance of nature. Anthropologists that study Native American tribes have made some intriguing discoveries. Many tribes used practices intended to enrich the fertility of their land, limit their consumption of resources, and engender a respect in their people for the land, so that it was viewed as sacred. Because of these contributions, many Anthropologists consider pre-Columbian Native Americans to have been vital for the health of their ecosystem. After the indigenous population of the Americas was severely decimated by disease and war briefly following the early European settlement, this integral feature disappeared. As a result, various species went extinct. The point of my telling this informative anecdote is to prove that mankind need not be a sore on the face of the earth. We are a unique and amazing creature that has a very important place in nature. We can emulate that legacy. If you prefer not to simplify to the extreme, more moderate things might help.

Even influential elites, like Steve Jobs, chose a way of life called minimalism. Minimalism has occasionally been made fun of, but the core ideas are quite noble. The point is to remove distractions and excesses from life in order to simplify one's schedule, reduce financial stress, and open up more time to focus on what is more important to you.

Here's a suggestion: when you've gotten tired of reading my words, take a look around your house. Is there any junk laying around? Anything you could sell to get rid of? Anything you could do without? Anything you could consolidate to make life simpler? Riches and lots of things are only appealing in theory, in reality they only mean more to worry about and more to lose. Happiness cannot be bought, happiness comes from within, having and fulfilling your purpose in life. In Japan and China, many people sleep on a mat on the floor, people without water heaters take cold showers, some only use one big pot in the kitchen that all members of the family share, one fork, one spoon, and one knife. Turn off the climate control and open the windows (too chilly? Put on a jacket!), wear the same two or three pairs of clothes all the time (like Albert Einstein did), etc. We're all a work in progress, the more we learn, the more we can get rid of. You can apply this to whatever extent you like; I understand that this would be considered extreme by many people in the Western world. The point is not just to have little stuff; the point is to have more time, thought, and energy for the worthwhile things in life.

Chapter 4: How to be Pleasant to be Around

I have always been a very opinionated person, but in the past, I took this to the extreme. When I was younger, I used to have very strong sentiments about everything, and I would always insist on my way, I would never compromise with people. Just like everything else, compromise can be a delicate balance; it is easy to go too far in one direction or the other. Some people go along with whatever others tell them, not thinking for themselves, or even if they do think for themselves, they are willing to sacrifice their beliefs to appease others. It is true, we need to have principles, and we need to stand by them. If we believed something but never defended it, we'd be pushovers, cowards, and hypocrites. Those who insist on their way no matter what are often extremely unpleasant to be around; they just are not kind people. That refusal to compromise used to be how I was, but later on, I realized that acting like that repelled people away from me and made me unhappy. So I started being more yielding, I started going along with what people said. More people started liking me at that point, but I soon found myself occasionally giving up my principles in order to make others happy. I had to learn to find a happy balance with this.

The rule of thumb I came to understand is: to compromise with others as much as you can without sacrificing your morals. When we compromise with family, friends, coworkers, and others, it will likely not be what we prefer, it will not be ideal in our opinion, but it will make both parties a little happier. Be willing to make self-sacrifices to help others, but never make a compromise that would hurt yourself. For example, I had a strong distaste for toxic chemicals, but some in my family did not share this sentiment. They often would use them to clean things. Instead of attempting to force them to never use chemicals, instead, I let them do what they want and I would clean and wash what was mine how I preferred to do it. Occasionally, I would attempt to reason with them on the matter; sometimes it worked, and sometimes it didn't.

Sometimes, a family member would ask me to use some kind of chemical cleaner to do a "deep clean," and as long as it would cause minimal harm to me and the environment (when used properly), I tried to meet them halfway.

If the other person will not meet you halfway, they want it exactly their way; you have the decision to make—will you stick by your stance or give in? The right decision depends very much on you, the other person, and the situation you are in. One thing to remember, though, is something many people would never think of. Slavery is not just owning another person or being owned by a master, it can also be when you are ruled by an authority. You may even be ruled by yourself. For my part, I don't want to be a slave to anyone or anything. I refuse to be ruled by addiction, fear, pleasures, or anything else. As long as in the course of your compromising you constantly maintain your sovereignty over your own choices, you are doing well. If people see that you are doing your best to please them and yet at the same time you are a principled, moral, virtuous person of integrity, they will trust you, respect you, and admire your indomitable spirit. You will indeed be a pleasant person to be around, a real joy.

The truth is, that if you do not like your life or your personality, you have nobody to blame. We often will experience some trauma when we're young, and this will imprint in our minds. We will keenly remember this moment, it will shape our beliefs about ourselves, and the pain of it still stings. This trauma will often change us and change our life course. If we have problems in life, we're depressed, we lack self-confidence, we have hatred, fear, addictions, etc.—we tend to blame it on something that happened to us or somebody. "I am how I am because of so-and-so or this-and-that." We are better than that. We don't need to live in the past, we need to let go of it. You are what you choose to be right now, nobody can make you what you are. If you're depressed, you don't need to tell yourself that you're happy—that would be a lie! Just tell yourself the truth: you have great potential, you have a purpose in life, you have the potential to be happy, to accomplish your purpose, to live your dream—but only you can make it happen. Others can help you along the way, your faith and spirituality can also help you, but ultimately you have to make the choices.

If we are not natural leaders, that is fine, we don't need to be the boss of other people, but we do need to lead ourselves. We need to train ourselves as you would train a dog. Our bodies have a mind of their own, the body loves to stay in its comfort zone, stay within the bounds of the familiar. Even if the familiar is depression and sorrow, the body fears changing that! But we have the power to change that, the choice is ours. Your body tells you: "I know this sugary cake will make you feel terrible, but it is pleasurable, it is comfort food, so do it—do it for me!" It asks of us things that are seldom for our benefit. The body can get into good habits, good comfort zones, but the body is like a dog, it needs training. Sometimes, when one of my dogs was younger, I would give her some food, I would move my hand towards the bowl, and she would growl at me. She was afraid I would take her treasure. So me and my family started training her. We would give her the food, take it away from her, make her sit and stay, then give it back. She had to learn to trust us: "Yes, Dog, I'll give you your food, I'll give you your toy, but you need to calm down, trust me, and sit and stay for a while." Our bodies are the same way, we need to train them and love them. Believe me, the body really is an intelligence of its own, but it can be dull witted, so it needs to learn to listen to us.

Another important aspect of being a pleasant person is your charisma. Speaking softly, slowly, and gently is vital for people to feel comfortable around you. We want to be approachable people, so we would be wise to be calm, patient, merciful, and choose our words wisely. A smile and eye contact are some other obvious habits to maintain as you deal with others. You may be a quiet, friendly person, but if you don't talk to people, don't smile, avoid eye contact, and so forth, you may seem standoffish and aloof.

While I was in High School and in a certain class, I was once assigned to mentor a new student. He was told by our teacher to ask me if he needed help, to have me show him the safety guidelines before using each tool, and in general, to let me guide his work. I didn't make an effort to go to him and help him; instead, I waited for him to come to me for help.

Ultimately, he didn't actually come to me at all and as a result, had a difficult time on a project and broke quite a few safety rules. The day after, I apologized for not going over to help him out, I was busy with my own project, and from then on, I made sure to show him the ropes. He had pride and said he had been fine without help, but clearly thereafter, he appreciated some assistance. I was very kind, patient, and helpful with the boy, but I wasn't approachable because I didn't make the first move to get to know him or befriend him.

In the same way, you may miss friendships, courtships, and possibly even a potential spouse if you do not seem approachable to those around you. You should radiate an aura of kindness, truth, and integrity. It should be apparent to whoever you may be around. You may seem different, in fact, you will be different because most people are not like that, but they will admire you and be most likely to go to you and trust you in times of trouble. Of course, that is easier said than done!

In order to ooze kindness from your very being, you cannot just act kind; you must be kind in every aspect of life. When you drive in traffic, do you get annoyed and honk somebody, even if they may "deserve" it? When you watch the news, and you see politicians' trickery, hypocrisy, and treachery, do you hate them? Do you judge those who feel differently than you, and believe different things than you? Even if you don't show it, do your friends or family annoy you, do you bottle up that distaste? Are you bitter about the trauma and hardships that have occurred in your life, even if they are severe? These are serious questions worth careful reflection on all our parts because our answers to them reveal something important. Are we actors of kindness or are we kind, even to ourselves?

As discussed in the first chapter, if you lack self-confidence and are unkind to yourself, that will be reflected in your dealings with others. Do not suppose that you can hide internal bitterness; and would you really want to? Lying is hard, it takes constant maintenance, caution, and fabrication to keep up. If we are not as we appear, why not either show our true self or change our true self? Fakery is no option. To become a new person, we have to unmake the old. That takes a profound change in our attitude and mentality that takes work. People are seldom ever handed a better personality on a silver platter, it usually takes work. Yes, some people have spontaneous, life-changing, experiences from some epiphany or revelation that fundamentally and immediately change their whole mind. Most of us have not been so lucky. We don't have to have a miracle to change.

We will all continue to be a work in progress so long as we live, so we might as well start now. Many people have to experience tragedy and sickness to realize there's more to life. If we start improving ourselves and searching for the truth now, we will save a lot of time and prevent many problems.

When we feel a certain way about somebody, be willing to share it. If you are thankful for what somebody did, tell them. Politeness also goes a long way (Yes sir, no sir, yes ma'am, no ma'am, please, thank you, good to meet you, how are you doing, have a good day, hold the door for others, wave, etc.). Apologize when you do wrong; you will be respected for it, and people will draw closer to you. And make your apology genuine; nobody likes "I'm sorry you feel that way." If you say that, you're really just putting the blame on them, and it will do no good whatsoever.

Listen more than you talk, unless the other person hardly says a word, in which case it might be a good idea to "break the ice." Laughing makes everyone around feel better, and the same with complimenting others when appropriate. They don't have to paint the Mona Lisa or build the Taj Mahal to be worthy of a compliment. If there is no conversation, why not start one? One thing to remember is that asking personal questions makes people feel uncomfortable and may even annoy them, so avoid that. Include outcasts and welcome less popular people and you will earn a friend easily. Hold back from giving too much criticism unless the person knows you well and you sincerely believe it will help them. Perform random acts of kindness, even to strangers; if you have a general attitude of kindness in your life, you will naturally see opportunities to help others.

In the same High School I previously mentioned, the same student under my mentorship was feeling poorly for a couple days in succession. The class was doing a study of the textbook, and there weren't enough copies for everybody, and this fellow didn't have one. I saw that he would have trouble paying attention without a book and that would only make it worse when we had to take the test afterwards, so I gave him my book and said I'd be fine just listening. The teacher complimented me on that, and everybody seemed to have a high respect for me thereafter. Also, he and I became friends after that.

Another thing to try is "when in Rome, do as the Romans do." This is an old-timey adage that still holds true just as much as when first it was first said. It indicates that we do best to appeal to people as much as possible, to follow their lead. You wouldn't want to be obstinate and refuse to adapt to your surroundings. At the same time, you wouldn't want to constantly compromise your principles in order to please others. Just like everything else, it's a delicate balance, and it's easy to go too far in either direction. When you sense a certain "vibe" or way of thinking on the part of someone you're around, try not to contradict them.

For example, I am extremely critical of technology, I like to live a simple, natural life with minimal distractions. I will make use of technology if there is some practical benefit to it, but I will not squander my time with it. I have observed that we live in an extremely unadventurous society; adventure is mostly found in fictional novels and television shows at this point. Why might that be? In the past, adventurers and explorers abounded. One reason is that people attend mandatory schooling, which teaches them to think inside the box, not outside the box, and they are encouraged to pursue a conventional and respectable career that will make them "successful," in other words, make lots of money. People now measure success not by happiness or helping others, but by their paychecks. But the thirst for adventure and wonder still burns within their hearts; how do they satisfy this urge? They watch television shows of other imaginary people living adventures. They live through the eyes of others, they use television and books as a crutch, as a way of experiencing adventure without having to leave their comfort zones and put forth the effort of living adventure for themselves. They content themselves with the imaginary, to the fictional. A few hundred years ago, fiction was unheard of for the most part, it was considered lying to write fiction. Now fiction abounds, and adventurous people diminish. Now, do not suppose I am advising you against all forms of media. The news is just plain mind-numbing and depressing at this point; each of us have enough of our own problems, we have no need to take the whole world's problems on our shoulders by having to hear about them. Pure entertainment is just a diversion, a waste of time. On the other hand, a book, television show, or something else that inspires us to live our own lives more fully—that is definitely worth our time! The internet, though it has many drawbacks and disadvantages, allows us to have almost the entire mass of accumulated human knowledge at our fingertips. With great power comes great responsibility; let's use it wisely and not frivolously.

Anyway, back to my original subject: an example of appealing to people. I have been wary of technology ever since childhood, but my friends at the time hardly shared that sentiment. They, as are many young people nowadays, were utterly addicted to technology. When I dealt with them, I had to be careful to express what I would and would not do without insulting their sensibilities. I admit it was often like walking on eggshells or thin ice. Eventually, I slowly parted ways with these friends because we had hardly anything in common. That made life easier for me, in my opinion. But having no friends can be hard, too! I later gained many friendships, though they were all much older than me, that was just fine. Old folks need help and have a lot of wisdom to share, I can assure you.

Tiptoeing around sensitive issues with people can be quite tiresome! If it's worth it to you, keep up that fellowship. But if your chosen company is more trouble than it's worth, you might want to consider going separate ways. If you have to be around certain people, workmates, for example, do your best to "kill them with kindness," and they might just stop bothering you.

Speaking of that subject, I have something else to share with you. In school, I was around people that cussed like sailors, no, worse than sailors. They used curses so frequently that it lost all meaning to them, it became something they used in order to supplement their limited vocabulary. I never felt the need to do so, myself. These kids also had no morals whatsoever, and not surprisingly, they were often depressed because they had no purpose in life. When the school year started, and I was in class with lots of new people, they would at first treat me poorly. I was no weakling, and I was quite capable of defending myself verbally or physically, but I was patient with them and refrained from retaliating. Pretty soon, they began to soften and reciprocate the same kind, quiet way with which I treated them. I could see the difference in how they treated their peers and how they treated me, they learned to calm down and mirror my personality. They were unaccustomed to being treated with compassion and concern, and this confused them. Each one of them was born a kind person, but they imitated others and learned to act harshly. At first, when I had just started school, I made the same mistake, but later, it occurred to me that I wasn't a sponge, I didn't have to soak up whatever was near me; from then on, I never saw fit to copy the behavior of others. I have often seemed strange because I don't conform, but I'm also admired when people begin to understand why I choose to live the way I do. As a freethinker, the insights I've gained have led me to do many odd things, but I don't care what's normal; if it helps me and my family live healthier and happier lives, I don't think I'll look back once I'm old and say: "Boy, do I wish I'd done what everybody else did." I aim to have no regrets, so I refuse to be tempted to give up my dreams. If you have dreams, a vision, especially one that is for the betterment of mankind, pursue it ferociously because it is not very likely to plop right in your lap without some effort.

We have lots of followers in our world and not enough leaders. Even many of our "leaders" are actually followers. Learn to be your own person, work well with others, and yet at the same time, be willing to take the initiative to be the first to do something, even if there's nobody else leading the way to show you how— learn as you go. If we have more inspiring, charismatic, incorruptible leaders in this world, we would have a much pleasanter world.

As I mentioned before, we often know who we really are, until we go to school. Let's take a lesson from the illustrious Mr. Mark Twain when he said, "I never let my schooling interfere with my education, " and, "We have not the reverent feeling for the rainbow that a savage has because we know how it is made. We have lost as much as we gained by prying into that matter," and finally, "Education consists mainly of what we have unlearned." Indeed, schooling is a different matter than education; education is made of personal interests that we research and therein find revelations. I have realized many wonderful things by simply pacing back and forth in the woods, pondering over a seemingly mundane subject. Also, as children, not to be rude, but we are basically savages. At that early age, we instinctively understand many things about what's really important, but we are soon taught right out of that wisdom. Decades later, we might realize that what we instinctively did as children were exactly what was good for us—now we have to try and repair the damage done by a lifetime of ignorance induced by schooling and baseless traditions. More important than learning and coming to know something is this instead: unlearning what we've been taught and realizing we know nothing at all! The more I learn, the more I realize I don't know. Anybody you see who thinks they are wise: do not trust them, that's actually the best sign that they are ignorant. If they really knew something, they would be open to the possibility that they may be wrong. A genius is not somebody that understands a lot, it is someone wise enough to understand that we all are quite stupid. One more quote from Mark Twain: "Thousands of geniuses live and die undiscovered—either by themselves or by others." We all have a lot of potential, we just have to figure out how to realize our full potential.

When you have that sense of purpose, that balance, that confidence, you will naturally be admired by most who meet you. Just remember to never hold yourself above others with a sense of superiority. If you act like that, just as soon as they begin to admire you, they'll flee from you. Quite frankly, keeping a balanced attitude is plain hard. We're like pendulums in an old grandfather clock that swing back and forth from one extreme to the other, never staying in the middle. Being distracted, busy, stressed, and multitasking can make it easy to fail to realize if we are off track. What I've found always helps me to step back and take an honest look at my life as an unbiased observer is just going into an isolated spot, pacing back and forth, talking to myself, and meditating. Focusing only on one thing at a time, the thing you're currently doing (in other words: living in the present moment). Disconnecting from the constant busyness is a necessity. If you make good habits like that, you'll make yourself and others happy.

Chapter 5: Understanding Psychology

Making friends and influencing people (hopefully in a positive way) are generally thought to be mostly physical activities. What we say to people, how we act, do we try and make the first move in friendship, are we approachable, etc. But there are also some mental aspects to human relationships that, if neglected, could cause us trouble.

As the saying goes, "no man is an island." Everybody needs some form of interpersonal connection, some support. Even a hermit off in the wilderness has a connection to the animals, plants, and land that he dwells in. Have you ever seen the film Cast Away with the actor Tom Hanks? In it, the protagonist, Chuck Noland, experiences a plane crash in the Pacific and is stranded on a remote island. He faces many challenges attempting to survive and keep his spirits up, but he lacks a friend. In order to create a friend for himself, he takes a volleyball he found in a package from the crash, then paints a face on it from his own blood, and names it "Wilson," which is the company name written on the ball. He views the ball like a companion and talks to it extensively; of course, essentially he's really just talking to himself, but our human, innate need for companions led him to pretend. This helped him maintain his sanity and keep up morale in such a seemingly bleak situation. Hopefully, none of us will have to face such a hardship as that, though, it honestly might be nice to be stranded on an island as long as you had something to keep you company—whether that be an animal, plant, or human. In any case, no matter how introverted we may be (I am definitely one such person), just stay isolated from people for a while, and you'll realize that you have a psychological need for companionship of some kind.

Friendship can have a strong effect on your health, for better or worse. Peer pressure is an ever-present stimulus that leads us to feel the need to conform to the behavior of those around us. A good and kind group of friends will inevitably encourage you to be happy, to be positive, to take care of yourself physically, and to have something to look forward to. On the other hand, the wrong crowd can be toxic for us, mentally and physically. We all rub off on each other, whether we like it or not, so choose your friends wisely.

Friends will offer us support when we face troubles and can help us get through our adversities. When at work, whatever your job may be, companions can make the time go faster, make us more content, and help us work faster. When I worked on a local man's farm, the same grouchy, but kind fellow I mentioned before: working alone every day would have been absolutely intolerable. He was exhausting to be around, and not just physically; he wore me down mentally to a nub. Now don't get me wrong, I liked the work for the most part, but on days where I worked there alone... Goodness, the time dragged on endlessly. I checked my watch and always found that little time had passed. Sometimes I would weed fields on my hands and knees in the Sun all day long, and not sparse weeds here and there, but whole jungles of vegetation taller than me! I love plants, but goodness, if pulling weeds is murder, then I committed genocide on a mass scale. My joints in my fingers, knees, back, neck, and feet would ache from the long maintenance of that awkward position, I would switch back and forth between squatting until neither were comfortable anymore—I just had to get used to being constantly uncomfortable, which was good for me. When I had company to talk to, to work alongside, to get some help from: the time sure flew then. I worked quicker, had more laughs, and enjoyed the day far more. If I didn't quite understand what I was supposed to do, my workmates would help me, and I would do the same for them. The workload was less overpowering if there were multiple people helping; many hands make the load light. As a literal example of that, we once were lifting a huge, solid oak banquet table, but quite a few hands lifted it up, and we each felt like we were lifting just a cardboard box! Ultimately, I view that early experience as a good one, and I'm no weakling, but I honestly couldn't have done it by myself. I suppose I could've done it alone, but I likely would've just quit after a while instead.

You know the expression: "It takes a village to raise a child." We in our Western culture are very independent, relatively speaking. Most families are made up of parents and their children. They have no community, no tribe. They often have never met their neighbors. Yes, we may have our religious community, our work community, our extended family, and our casual friends, but our lives are very compartmentalized, very separate. In the old days, the people you worshiped were the same that lived side by side with you, worked with you, danced with you, sang with you, and loved you. Even their future spouses would be found in their tribe or village, everything and everyone they needed was within a close distance to them. This was a necessity in a world without cars and grocery stores, people needed each other.

Now, you can make money doing a job in an office, that money is sent in imaginary numbers to your bank account, you buy your needs and wants in a store or through the Internet, and you probably produce very little of your own food and do not really need your neighbors. You may be used to that lifestyle, but consider the possible advantages of a supportive community. We would be self-sufficient, we would pollute our lands far less, we would have less stress, etc., etc., etc.. Just think about that for a second, how would your life and the lives of your beloved family members benefit from a real community, a tribe? It may take a whole village to raise a child in the best way possible, but that's impossible if you have no village in the first place. Try to build a community, your own tribe, you don't have to make big changes if you don't want to, but just start being more friendly with your neighbors and see what happens.

If you want to find friends, but don't know how I'll give a few suggestions. Many people use social media, and they may have many online "friends." But they likely never spoke to many of these people, and certainly never met them face-to-face. Social media gives people the feeling of being "connected" while never actually having any personal connections. If you content yourself with friends you talk to with buttons, you may lose many of the benefits of real friends. Social media, I'm sure, can be useful for finding like-minded people, especially if your interests are obscure or unusual, but please, try to use social media only as a way of finding people to meet—don't just be penpals. Some other ways of finding friends may be to go to some local religious meeting, volunteer at some helpful community project, join a club, offer to help your neighbors with yard work (especially if they're elderly or unwell), or make friends with the people you work with.

It's no easy task to just go and start up a conversation with a stranger, so it might be easier to focus on being friendly with the folks you're around every day. But if you do want to strike up a conversation with a stranger, here's some basic pointers: smile, look them in the eye, compliment them on something to put them at ease, maybe ask them a question (if you don't think it will make them uncomfortable—don't put people on the spot), have a sense of humor, and if appropriate, perhaps ask them if you both could exchange contact information. In a small, country town, this process will be much easier because people are usually at ease there anyway.

If you already have friends and would like to keep the friendship thriving, here's a few things to keep in mind. Spend time with them. Don't suppose you can plant the seed of friendship, walk away, come back after a long time, and expect that plant of friendship to have grown. Friendships are what we make them, as such, we need to invest time, care, and effort. If we expect them to treat us with care, we have to treat them with care. Trust is also a necessity, but building trust can be hard. People generally begin to trust each other when they go through hard times together, they support each other all the way, and no temptation causes them to betray each other; their loyalties are tested, and they prove true every time, through thick and thin, bitter and sweet. But if we only have casual friendships and we do not rely on each other for anything whatsoever, how can we have such close friendships? Well, honestly, nothing can approximate going through hard times together. There is a special attachment there that cannot be imitated.

Did you ever see the Lord of the Rings trilogy of films based on J. R. R. Tolkien's masterfully-made books? If so, you'll recall that throughout the story, the protagonist, Frodo, and his friend, Sam, became progressively closer as they leaned on each other during their long, perilous, and fearful journey. At one point, Frodo attempted to go off on his own to finish the worst part of the trek; he didn't want anybody else to have to bear his burden with him. Despite this, his dear friend Sam chased after him and insisted upon going with him—they'd come this far together, and they would finish together: there was no other way. Later, near the end, climbing the blistering hot slopes of an evil mountain and hiding from the eye of their great enemy, you can perceive the way that the sheer intensity of facing all these hardships had drawn them together. The best of friends can only be produced by intimately living side-by-side, in good times and bad times (which is why, when such a relationship fails, it is far more devastating than a more superficial one).

Nonetheless, being there for your friend, even in the little things, for a long time—will lead you to a close friendship. And not to be negative, but in the worsening, dark, bleak, and divided world around us, we may just end up going through some hard times. Economic concerns, wars overseas, unusual illnesses—we've already experienced those. But let's be real, most of us have faced no real cataclysm, no severe calamity, no mass catastrophe. We have our individual and family problems, but nothing like what could happen. What is probably about to happen... So let's be thankful for this, and though I'd never wish a worldwide catastrophe on anybody, if such does come to pass, I have no doubt that we will band together and unite to face whatever comes.

The increasing divisiveness and contention between those of differing opinions in our society is becoming more polarized all the time—and that may affect our friendships. It may be hard to relate to someone of a drastically different mentality. Of course, we should be civil and kind to anybody we meet, but we may choose not to pursue a friendship with those who think too differently from ourselves. Such relationships can last a little while, but the whole time, each of you will be walking on eggshells to avoid insulting the other person or sharing your personal opinions that would bother your friend. Eventually, such relationships universally tend to lead to estrangement and separation. Now, don't suppose that just because someone has differing views than you, that this person must be evil—that would be unreasonable and imbalanced on your part to make that brash assumption. Consider how their family, background, and upbringing may have led to their views. You may not agree, but at least you should learn to understand where they're coming from.

In particular, politics, religion, and now personal medical preferences (you probably know what I mean, though I don't want to get into detail) are big controversies; they can be very divisive topics. It may be wise to avoid discussing them unless you know you are with a like-minded person or group.

Politics used to be a dry subject regarding economics and suchlike, the kind of thing that old men in black suits would discuss in a dimly-lit board room while smoking their pipes. The point is that it was not an exciting topic that the average person would be interested in, and certainly young people used to care little or nothing for politics. In the past, most people agreed on what their political, common goal was, but they just disagreed on how to accomplish that goal. Nowadays, things have taken a different turn: politics are now based on moral, religious, and scientific issues, and nobody even has a common goal. I know you've probably heard something like this before, but what do people usually say next? Usually they say something along the lines of: "I wish people could just agree on things and believe in common sense. You know, I pretty much wish they'd agree with me." I will not say that to you because that would defeat the whole point of condemning our polarized world. If I said that the solution to our political problems was everybody agreeing with my views, wouldn't that just make the problem worse?

The problem is not just the polarization of politics, but also the fact that people can't seem to understand that they don't have to hate "the other side" or "the bad guys." We are not in a sports competition, we're not in a literal military war (yet), though we certainly are in an intellectual war. Let me warn you, from a thorough study of history, you will undoubtedly find that our society is following the telltale steps towards collapse, anarchy, and war. "A house divided cannot stand," and I guarantee you that for numerous societal, cultural, religious, and environmental reasons, our society is destined towards calamity if something does not suddenly change. I'm sorry to say that, but we are not immune to history, the modern world follows the same age-old patterns, but I want you to know that this is our choice: we can change it. That change would start with our refusal to demonize those who feel differently than us, our refusal to treat them as enemies, and our willingness to move outside the bounds of our "team" to do what we believe to be right and to make friends. Our goal is to work towards the common good, not to stick with our "team" no matter what, and choose to hate those who disagree with us. We can make friends with those who disagree with us. The question is: are you willing to?

Tribalism is an unusual topic in sociology and psychology. On one hand, we observe that people thrive better when they have the support and fellow feeling of a tribe or clan, but on the other hand, unfortunately, tribalism, in certain types of societies, can create competition and strife between different groups which leads to violence, hatred, warfare, and petty feuds. We can see that in our society. Even with something so trivial, in the grand scheme of things, as team sports can pit people against each other to the point of violence. I once heard of a fan of one American football team who heard a nearby fan of a different team cheering, which angered the former individual to an extreme degree. He then proceeded to approach that other fan and brutally beat him to a pulp, almost killing him. Of course, he was prosecuted and jailed. Honestly, let's think about that for a second. You understand that

American football teams are franchises that have team members from all over the country, most are not even from the area that the team claims to represent. In addition, teams will occasionally move to a far away location if it appears to be more profitable, proving that the team is just a business and not in any way loyal to any particular place. And yet people can become so obsessed with watching these games and rooting for their team that it tears their friendships apart.

Where I lived as a child, I would frequently see signs on many people's doors that said: "A house divided," and it would show a picture underneath split in half, with each side showing the emblem of one of the two popular football teams in that area. I actually would see kids in school occasionally coming to blows over this issue. I will not mince words over this: such an attitude is insane, idiotic, and inexcusable. In all honesty, fans of team sports tend to be more hateful towards the other side than the actual sports players are! The reason for that is that football is just a job to them, maybe even a passion, but as they personally know many players from other teams, they do not feel the need to treat them with contempt (though of course there are exceptions to this when a brawl occurs). The fans are not even playing the game, they're just watching others play it, so the great mental investment that fans put into their team is unreasonable, illogical, and unfounded in reality. I do not mean to insult those who feel this way, but our world has enough real hatred and controversy that it seems silly to create imaginary controversy over team loyalty in sports. But psychologically speaking, we all have a desire to have a community of like-minded people, a tribe, a group to support us and work together for the common good.

As I mentioned before, because of our modern lifestyle, our communities are fragmented; our church or religious community is seldom made up of the same people as our work community, our work mates are seldom ever our next-door neighbors, and our next-door neighbors are seldom our best friends or family. This separated and fragmented society is symptomatic of the mental trauma, confusion, and psychological imbalance that modern life has afflicted us with. But we do not have to be "victims," we can choose whether we follow the crowd in groupthink or whether we follow our principles like free people.

Remember though, we can try to do it alone, and we may not do so shabby, but we cannot reach our full potential without the support of others. Perhaps you've heard of the historical Mountain Men who left "civilized" society in the 1800s in order to roam free over the Rocky Mountains and other wildlands, hunting, trapping, and selling furs for what little money they wanted in order to buy items and ammunition. In books and films, Mountain Men are often portrayed as solitary hermits that lived alone and were grim, grimy, and grumpy all the time (Jeremiah Johnson is one example). In reality though, most often, Mountain Men traveled in groups or bands for safety and comradery.

Imagine getting injured in the vast wilderness all alone, you may be able to save yourself and you may not, but with a group, you are much more likely to enjoy life and actually live a long time. In addition to their group, Mountain Men would also trade extensively with Native American tribes, marry women from a tribe, and even occasionally join the tribe and live among them. They were not often lone wolves. In addition, hunting some large game such as bear, elk, and buffalo was far easier with many people. I can assure you, if you're hunting a bear or it charges you and you are forced to defend yourself, it's very unlikely that even the most powerful rifle will drop the bear instantaneously. Even if the bullet creates a fatal wound, the bear will usually live long enough to maul you, too. Successful bear hunting is far more attainable and appealing when there are many hunters who all fire together to increase their chances of getting some meat and coming out alive. Sorry, I know most of you all likely have never nor ever intended to hunt a grizzly bear, but I hope that relating this little anecdote about Mountain Men will help you see the merits of working as a team—it may mean your life in dark times ahead.

On a more positive note, also quite important to a successful friendship is humor. A stoic, dry, bleak-faced person may not be enjoyable to be around, whereas somebody with a strong sense of humor will be able to make people feel comfortable and relaxed around him/her and will be able to make hard times more tolerable by finding amusement in the little things. That's not to say you should be a clown all the time; somebody that can't take anything seriously is not a good candidate for a person to throw your cares on, to confide in, because such a goofy person wouldn't take your problems seriously. As with everything, it's a delicate balance. You should be able to make light of things, lighten the mood, and make life seem less overwhelming, while at the same time, you need to be able to listen attentively when your friend is in distress. Just listening is often the best way to help a distraught person. If you attempt to give them advice, only do so after listening until they're finished talking, then softly and gently give them useful advice—do not give advice that minimizes their problem.

By experience, I can tell you, and you've probably seen for yourself, that telling somebody to "calm down" is a terrible idea. Those words inevitably have the opposite effect on all but the mildest of people, it "riles them something terrible." Anger and severe perturbations will ensue if you take that wrong step, and seldom will any apologies soothe them. Also, when somebody confides in you about some problem or tragedy, I wouldn't recommend saying to them: "I understand." Their mental response is generally: "No, you don't understand; nobody can understand what I'm going through unless they've gone through it," and they likely find it difficult to conceal their annoyance at your untimely comment. Most of the time, just crying with them (if you are able), listening to them talk, and soothing them by putting your hand on their shoulder, holding their hand, or hugging them are the best options. In order to figure out the right response in each situation, try and imagine what it would feel like from their point of view, observe their body language, and listen to their tone of voice in order to feel for them (pity/sympathy), or better yet: feel with them (empathy). If you can accurately perceive how they're feeling, you will be more likely to respond appropriately. I know it may feel uncomfortable for you to comfort a grieving person, you may not know what to say, but that's not necessarily a bad thing: you might not have to say anything.

Of course, when it comes to touching somebody to comfort them, you'd probably only want to do that with friends and family you are very familiar with, though, if you come across as sincere and empathetic, even a complete stranger may sometimes appreciate it. Ultimately, it all comes down to your ability to read people's emotions, so practice that. For me, I'm not one to frequently make conversation with strangers, and certainly not hug a stranger! I'm far more comfortable and open with people than I used to be, but it's still a challenge—it's easy to stay within the confines of our "comfort zone." If you feel the same way, you're certainly not the only one. We would probably find it easier if we grew up in some remote and self-sufficient village or tribe where everybody knows each other from birth to death. I would be more comfortable in that situation, quite honestly, but few of us are, and if you were in that situation, you probably wouldn't be reading this book, now would you?

I suppose the key is to find like-minded, open, frank, honest, and unembarrassed people that easily show their feelings and happily accept them from others as well. That's easier said than done, though, right? I have found such people on occasion, but as I said, if what you currently have in life is not what you ultimately, really want, then you can't expect to find what you want and be able to stay in your comfort zone. If you could achieve your goals while living exactly as you are right now, then you would have already reached those goals by now. Sorry, but to follow your dreams, answer those deep and nagging questions within your soul, and fulfill the desires of your heart (the things you long for deep down without being aware of them), you are going to have to get out of your comfort zone. I repeat: escape your comfort zone. You are likely limiting yourself within a box of your own making, a prison of sorts. And you "can't escape a prison you don't know you're in."

In order to figure out if you've been living a lie, living an endless, redundant, repetitive, and futile rat race—you'll have to explore possibilities you never considered before. If you wish to seek the truth, you must at least once in your life question everything. Take nothing for granted. As a wise man once said, "It is the mark of an educated mind to be able to entertain a thought without accepting it." I was once told by a very wise and dear friend of mine: "The more one learns, the less one truly knows. Those who claim to know almost everything are clearly mistaken by the very fact they could believe such a thing. Our world, our reality is beyond all fathoming; those who reject the great mystery in it are misled." As a final quote for this little book, I shall take from an unlikely source, Star Wars, as the fictional character Obi-wan

Kenobi said, "Everything is true from a certain point of view." Would you humor me? Just think about that quote seriously for a bit...

This may be an overwhelming thought for you. You might think: "how can I tell what's true and what isn't, then?" The goal is not to find the truth, no one can find all truth, but to be constantly seeking truth, being content with the fact that we will never find it all, nor even be able to undeniably confirm any belief without a doubt. Our love for each other and our love for the truth, whatever that may be, is what binds us together, for to love is our only purpose in life.

Conclusion

I would like to sincerely thank you for making it through to the end of How to Make People Do What You Want. I hope it was informative and will provide you with some of the tools you need to achieve your goals, whatever they may be.

The next step is to apply the information. Reading alone is not enough to change your life, and one book alone is not enough to make you wise. We must keep searching if we would like to even begin to find the truth and gain freedom from it.

Therefore, in order to help you remember what you've read in this book, I'll give you a good summary of everything we discussed together. Do you remember how I told you in this book's introduction that I would spare you from having to read a long explanation of what you were about to read? Well, in my opinion, a long preview is useless, but a thorough review afterward helps cement what we learn in our minds (so information doesn't go in one ear and out the other). So please pardon me, but here is the part where I will go into a detailed review for you.

In Chapter 1: Develop Balanced Self-Confidence, we discussed how you can learn to think of yourself in a balanced way: neither think too much of yourself nor too little. How can you apply that? Serve others. If you live to help others, serve them, you cannot be insignificant because you will be an invaluable help to those around you, and you will be greatly appreciated. At the same time, because you are a servant, not a boss, you will not be corrupted by power, you will remain humble and self-sacrificing. Wealth and power tend to corrupt all but the most virtuous people, so do not wish to be rich and do not crave power. You will regret it later.

Your goal should be to have what you need and maybe a little extra to give to those around you. If you have big plans, you'll have big needs, but don't let your life become too complicated, or you may lose sight of what's important.

How can you serve others, though? Give spur-of-the-moment gifts to your friends and family; you don't need a holiday to do that. Help your neighbors out, especially the elderly and sickly, perhaps cooking for them, help them clean their house, help them grow their garden, or take them to appointments. You will have an inner joy from this as giving is better than getting.

Try and volunteer locally or perhaps even far away. Maybe pick up the litter along your road, help a local farmer (and hear some good stories and learn a thing or two), or whatever works for you. When opportunities come to do something new, something helpful, don't pass it up. It's rare that people regret doing good but often that they regret doing nothing at all.

If you have something good, you are obligated to share it with others, not just keep it to yourself. If you are feeling down, and you build others up with encouragement, surprisingly, you'll find yourself encouraged, too. We are not meant to live only for ourselves, so working together builds us all up.

Your lack of self-confidence may be from an old wound deep down from your childhood. The poison and festering infection in that wound may need drawing out. Drawing trauma back to the surface will be uncomfortable, but how much more uncomfortable would it be if you left it unresolved. Going to a therapist might help. And keep in mind that going to a therapist does not mean that you are insane. Really, we're all insane to an extent, it's just a matter of how much so. But you don't necessarily need outside help, you can try different forms of meditation to help you resolve your mental scars. Many people benefit from the Tapping technique, or EFT; perhaps you could do some research into these modalities.

For most people, though, too much confidence or too little confidence stems back to a disconnection from reality. They cannot see themselves as they really are. Engaging with hard manual labor outside is a good way to re-engage with the real world. The Amish have the right idea in that regard, hard work, they believe, keeps them grounded in practicality and keeps them down-to-earth. I've had some dealings with the Amish, and I've never yet met one that was unrealistic or haughty. In fact, the religion of the Amish is actually based very much upon humility. Their choice to remain separate from the modern world makes their communities reliant upon each other, and as such, they are held accountable for their actions. If an Amishman acts like a jerk, he will lose his reputation, and that will cause him trouble. If your boss acts like a jerk, you just have to grin and bear it—there's likely nobody who has the authority to set your boss straight. An Amish community must be interdependent because they truly do need each other. Our modern technological world gives each of us the illusion of independence, but we are very much reliant on others. Yes, you can work your job, make money, go to the store and buy what you want—nobody is helping you do these things. But at the same time, if it were not for modern industry: the factories producing your food, water, electricity, this book, and the items you use for your daily life, you would be sunk. So, in reality, our world is more interconnected than ever before, but unlike in the past, we are no longer interconnected as much with nature. Instead, we are interconnected with the industrial economy.

Many people, called homesteaders, gain pride by becoming self-sufficient in their needs so that they are not at the mercy of others to provide their very lifeline. This can give you confidence and a release from fear. If the world collapsed around you, which is not really so unlikely a scenario nowadays, you would be just fine. Maybe you'd have to be a little more careful about conserving your resources, but life would go on for you much as it did before. If you want to have the ultimate self-confidence, I urge you to rekindle your connection with nature.

Humility and a reasonable self-confidence are due to a recognition of your reality. Any imbalance in your life will affect your self-esteem in some negative way, so we do best to continually examine ourselves, observe and evaluate our actions, speech, and thoughts, along with taking the time to have solitude, peace, quiet, and stillness so as to have a clear mind and reassess our current trajectory in life. We cannot suppose that by treating life like a race that we'll be very happy.

On occasion, I've met people that are so busy, live so hectically, so over-occupied that they do not even understand the concept of patience or calm reflection. School Children nowadays are glued to their phones at every opportunity, and their use of technology is quite frivolous, just for pure entertainment. To talk to them about the beauty of nature would likely elicit a scoff from them, and they'd return to their familiar technology. Living in a virtual reality is a good way to, well, lose touch with reality. Oftentimes, kids will become so obsessed with devices that it will seem to them to be their whole life. As such, when somebody says something unkind to them on social media, it frequently causes them to fall into the bottomless pit of despair, get depressed, and sometimes, sadly, even commit suicide. The internet is their world, their life, and so a simple insult, rather than causing them to fight back, often leads them down a dark path. Our lives need to be based on more than one thing, one aspect, and we need to develop a thick skin that lets insults bounce off us without bothering us. That's easier said than done for somebody who wasn't raised that way, but doing hard manual labor will quickly change that. In the same way, as hard work causes us to develop calluses, which help our hands to be tougher and more resilient, in the same way, hard manual labor has the effect of making us more emotionally tough and resilient. If you live in the city, that'll be a challenge, but I encourage you to find some way of working hard, not just exercising, but actual, practical work. Like farming, gardening, digging, raising livestock, lifting heavy things, and so on. You may have to leave the city every once in a while to do such things, but you'll be better off for it.

In Chapter 2: Persuasive Techniques, First Impressions, and Body Language, we discussed how to present yourself in a way that makes you seem respectable. This applies to business situations, job interviews, casual conversations, and all interpersonal activities. You may be respectable or you just plain may not be, but if you give the clear impression that you are incompetent, weak, uninformed, awkward, or otherwise, whoever may be talking to you will not find you very appealing. That could cost you a job, your respect, your reputation, your romance, and your friendships. Good parents teach their children manners, common courtesy, politeness, decorum, and common sense from birth. But some parents, for whatever reason, may neglect to do so, perhaps their own parents never taught them manners, or perhaps their children just didn't absorb their parents' instruction. All I ask is this: if you have children or plan to have them, give them a good head start in life by teaching them manners. It's much harder to change your habits once they're established, so it's better to start early.

You may think that manners are silly and unnecessary, and I agree, many Victorian-like manners are absurd and baseless. And if you want to have a more relaxed family environment at home, by all means you can forgo them, but still show your kids how to act in public. Your kids may be very intelligent, very kind, very capable young people, but other people will never know it if your children seem boorish, crude, and rude. I am definitely a free thinker; I disagree with many, no, most of our modern traditions and customs, but I still know how to present myself as an appealing and mannerly person to strangers who do not understand my mentality. Once you and your children get to know people better, you can absolutely act more relaxed around them, it's only natural, but manners serve an important purpose in our society: to give the signal to others that they are respected. Don't withhold that respect from others; you and they will regret it.

The next step is to start meeting people, if this applies to you, in order to test your manners out. Your skills will increase the more you practice. I have found that the things I generally used to be nervous about: talking to strangers, job interviews, crowds, and whatnot—the anticipatory fear was worse than the actual experience. I'd always come away feeling comfortable and proud of myself; my fears were not well-founded. The things I fear, and the things you fear—they're not real, the fears are of your own making. At this point, all my fears have dissipated: I no longer fear death, nor pain, nor people, nor danger, nor being alone, nor starvation, nor failure, nor any potential misfortune. I enjoy life for what it is, and not what it is not. If I die, so be it, I prefer to live, but death is not something to be feared. The only thing I still fear is being trapped. The things you fear may well happen, so do your best to prevent them, but don't live in constant dread and desperation—if you do that, you won't be able to enjoy your current life either. Just learn to say: "So be it," to any misfortune that befalls you, "this too shall pass." We'll cross that bridge when we get there, as they say. So don't fear doing new things, in this case, meeting people.

Also, start treating your family and friends better right now. This will show you that you are capable of being more respectful, enjoy being so, and that others like it, too. It might seem odd at first to change your behavior with your family, especially if you've been habitually acting the same way for a long time, and other people might think you're acting odd, but don't misinterpret that—they do prefer respect, and so do you. Who doesn't want respect? But to get respect you have to give respect. Yes, you have to earn it, it is not a right but a privilege.

One of the foremost problems in our society is a sense of entitlement. Many people believe that they deserve special treatment, or they deserve a free handout, or they deserve respect or love without being respectful and loving to others. Such people will inevitably and eventually find that this is not how life works. This selfish, lazy, and brat-like attitude is symptomatic of the fundamental nature of our current Western society. We have things easy, really easy. You likely don't have to draw water from a well, or fill up a barrel from a spring and haul the water back to your house with a yoke on your shoulders. No, you twist a knob, and the water miraculously appears from the spigot. You probably don't have to hunt, garden, or gather wild plants; you may choose to do so as a hobby, but you don't have to because a quick trip to the grocery store and you'll have everything you want, whenever you want it. Life is too easy nowadays, and it makes people weak, makes them reliant upon others, and makes them feel entitled to receive things they never worked for. Think of your ancestors, though, just a hundred or so years ago, when those things were not options. When people only reaped from hard work. If you didn't work, for the most part, you didn't eat.

History shows us that easy, luxurious living makes weak people, weak people become decadent and demanding and have a sense of entitlement, these weak people create a weak society, and this weak society soon collapses into war, famine, and anarchy. It's happened again and again throughout history, is currently happening in certain countries around the world, and could soon happen in your country if something doesn't change quickly. We rely upon a system that is so fragile and so intricate that even a slight malfunction or natural disaster could spell the end of this age. If we rely upon this technology to supply everything we need, we will be utterly sunk if we lose it.

My point is not to go off on a rant about potential future disasters, but my point is that we can choose to continue being weak, but we may be forced to rapidly toughen up or die pretty soon. On the other hand, if we learn to be strong now, to get over our squeamishness, to learn how to take care of ourselves, to change our way of life to one that allows us to live more independently of the establishment—if we get tough now, we will be ready for whatever comes. And it doesn't have to be a worldwide catastrophe, it could be a loved one's death, losing your job, a divorce or break-up, a severe disease, an accident, or anything else. Why wait till then? If we toughen up and get calluses now, when things may be easy, we will be able to deal with worse hardships in the future.

Do not demand special treatment from others or even the government. You may call it your "rights," and that may be true, but truly examine yourself deeply for a moment, ask yourself:

"have I really earned these rights, do all people deserve them, are they really unalienable rights, or am I just asking for special treatment?" Many people ask for special treatment because they feel they were oppressed or held down, maybe so, but maybe they're just using that as an excuse to get a free handout. Where I grew up, I actually did meet plenty of people who were abused, mistreated, and oppressed, but I never heard them asking for free handouts and special treatment. They were tough people, strong people, hard-working people. They were ashamed to receive charity from anyone they thought was giving pity. These were the older people. On the other hand, our younger generations, whose parents often pampered and made excuses for them, they live in unprecedented luxury and ease and legal equality. But all that is not enough, their appetites are insatiable, greedy for handouts and praise, while getting rageful and bruised at the slightest put-down. These loud and boisterous voices that we hear speaking are not the voice of reason, reality, or even the majority. Those of you who belong to the pampered sort, don't suppose I mean to bother you, but consider taking this advice: turn that "belong to the pampered sort" into "belonged to that pampered sort." We can change, in fact, we will have to change. Times are getting no easier, and sooner or later, we're going to have to toughen up. If we wait till we have to, we'll make life harder for ourselves, whereas if we start getting tough now, we'll sail smoothly, or at least a good bit smoother than most people, through the raging, tempestuous seas of our coming hard times ahead. A big part of getting tough is actually earning what we get, not just believing we already deserve it. So start now: give respect to get respect.

In Chapter 3: Empathy, we went over various methods for you to learn how to feel for others. Sometimes this can be hard to learn. I know a man who is a good example: he truly believes he is a kind, balanced, yielding, normal, and reasonable person, but most everybody that knows him disagrees. Now don't get me wrong, he can be fun to be around on occasion, but staying with him for any extended period of time tends to be increasingly unpleasant. Now, mind you, he is oblivious to this.

My point is that even if you truly believe you are empathetic and kindhearted, you do well to carefully examine yourself. Now, living alone for a long time often makes people self-absorbed, not necessarily entirely selfish, but more focused on oneself than would be proper. Some people are just delusional, they live in a fantasy, they see themselves or a certain situation a certain way, and nothing you could say or do would change their mind. I suppose the problem is often when you give people power and authority over others. We've all seen corruption in politics, on all sides, and there's the old adage: "Power tends to corrupt, and absolute power corrupts absolutely." When we have no one to answer to, we can "get too big for our britches." For example, a father who rules over his family like a king, taking no input from his wife and treating his children in a dictatorial manner. Now, don't suppose a wife couldn't act the same way, in fact, nowadays, that seems even more frequent—matriarchy. But, on the other hand, imagine a primitive tribe such as our dearly beloved Native Americans in the past. Such tribes share everything, including power, so a parent or pair of parents do not have exclusive authority over their children or anybody else for that matter.

For example, a frequent societal system among various Native American tribes was the matrilineal system. Lineage and clan membership (similar in some respects to the Western concept of surnames) were based on a child's mother, instead of the father, the opposite of what is done in most modern societies. The children would be loved, cared for, and given advice by all the older people. The men had elders and war chiefs that would lead in battle based on their proven courage and prowess in previous battles. At the same, the men did not make all the decisions, for the war chiefs ultimately answered to the older women, the grandmothers. Do you see how that system is similar to a democratic government, with checks and balances? Whereas in many households nowadays, we often have a particular parent who is very dominant, and who makes most of the decisions independently. There is no higher authority in the family. This is one reason why there are more controversies in modern families, because all authority is placed in the hands of one or two people, as opposed to a whole tribe or village community.

My point is that when we have to work with others and others have to work with us, we are all better kept in our place. We are less likely to become selfish, and selfishness is the foremost enemy of empathy—how can you be keenly aware and concerned for others' welfare when your priority is only yourself?

The primary catalyst for change in our habits is contemplation. If we take the time to reflect on our day, ponder over the good and bad points, we'll see how to improve next time. Life is really just one continuous school, with plentiful lessons. If we ignore the lessons, then we cannot benefit from them and learn to improve ourselves in order to fulfill our purpose in life. If life keeps getting harder and harder, maybe we should consider that as a message to go in a different direction; don't stick to a plan just for the sake of it, be willing to adapt to curves along the way. Life does not have to be hard, if it is, there's something wrong and it should be our goal to figure out how to correct it and, in turn show others what we've found. We can learn the easy way or the hard way. We are often too thick-skulled to learn the easy way, so we'll experience hardships in life. The only good use for misfortunes is to learn from them and to do better the next time, but if we don't learn, then the hardship was all for nothing, it was entirely futile, it was to no avail, it did not benefit us whatsoever. If we sit in silent contemplation, much will occur to us that our active and manic minds will never reveal otherwise. If we see a way to improve our way of treating others, then imagine yourself doing it, play it out in your mind, practice it, then you'll do better when the real situation faces you. Learn to go into deep meditation so as to access our subconscious mind, to correct any imbalances that may be there, and reprogram our minds to think straight.

Another resource that you're currently making use of is books. Benefit from the skills and accumulated knowledge of others. I'm sorry to tell you, but I'm not your man for that! I just want to start you in a good direction. I do not claim to be the most experienced or wise of people, I'm not even close to the top of the list. Some extremely insightful and useful books I would recommend to you that you might not have heard of before are: How to Break the Habit of Being Yourself by Dr. Joe Dispenza and The Alchemist by Paulo Coelho, and plenty more besides. I highly recommend those two. Of course, religious texts, such as the Bible, are far more insightful, but they do take a lot of careful study, and not all of your studies will be especially interesting, so you have to be ready for that. If you are accustomed to immediate gratification of your desires, then careful study is not for you because it may take years to even begin to understand complicated subjects, let alone actively researching and contributing to them. Patience is a virtue, indeed.

Patience is also a major virtue with regards to empathy. Someone might unknowingly or even knowingly annoy you, and without patience, you'll be likely to lash out at them. Try to understand people's actions and attitudes from their point of view, do not impose your own mentality upon them. It would be foolish to suppose people all think the same way as us, we all have a different upbringing, background, heritage, culture, spirituality, lifestyle, and genetics for that matter.

To learn patience, try doing long projects, try building something, watching the wind in the treetops, practicing martial arts, learning an instrument, and so forth. Anything that would force you to slow down, relax, not expect immediate results, and learn to reach goals little by little rather than all at once. Life is often compared to a race, but it would be better to compare it to a journey. It's not a competition, it doesn't really matter how long you take to get where you're going, it's an experience, not a destination. The biggest part of improving yourself, in this case, becoming more empathetic, is to first understand there's room for improvement, that you could do better, and then to simply desire to improve and intend to do so. Intention alone, when strong and sustained consistently, is enough to lead us in the right direction. Now, an effort will be involved, and you will have to work for your goals, but the ferocious intention is a force to be reckoned with.

To accomplish anything, especially a change in personality, grit and courage are necessary. Grit to persevere and bust through the roadblocks. Courage to step outside the unknown, out of your comfort zone. Doing things that are uncomfortable can get you accustomed to bravery and grit. Wim Hof, if you have heard of him, is a perfect example of this. The man ran a marathon in the Arctic with nothing but shorts, and also frequently dunks himself in the coldest water possible. This has been proven to have a variety of benefits, including reduced inflammation, positive mood, energy, and mental clarity. You may not be ready to hop into an ice bath quite yet, but at least try this: after you've lathered up with suds in the shower, turn the water cold as it gets and thoroughly rinse off. There's no denying it—it's extremely uncomfortable and shocking, but it is absolutely invigorating afterward! Try keeping your breathing calm, slow, and relaxed; otherwise, you will begin to hyperventilate in shock. As long as you keep your breathing calm, it will be tolerable. Honestly, try it, it truly does make you feel good.

With all this, you might be wondering: "What does all this have to do with the subject of this book?" The answer: anything that helps you feel better, look better, have mental clarity, and toughens you will help you to overcome bad habits, start creating good ones, become more confident, more kind, more peaceful, more content, more sociable, more adventurous, more skilled, more curious, and just plain more balanced all around.

In Chapter 4: How to be Pleasant to be Around, we outlined how to appeal to people and become a universally attractive person. By attractive, I don't just mean your physical appearance, I know plenty of pretty people who I wouldn't trust to fry an egg. Appearance is part of it, I suppose, if you're plain ugly then it'll be hard for people to be attracted to you, even if you have a nice personality. It's possible to overlook appearance, and it's a wonderful thing to do so, but it can be hard to do at times. But take heart, my friend, there really are very few truly ugly people, and I highly doubt you are one of them, whatever you may think about yourself. We may not all be fit for a Greek marble statue, but then again not too many people are. It is far more important to focus on your inner beauty, the kind that really matters. A magnet might not be the prettiest thing you ever did see, but two magnets pointed in the right way towards each other will have an irresistible attraction.

In order to be that attractive, we need to learn to appeal to people. There are many kind, sincere, well-intentioned, and wise people I know that simply don't know how to present themselves to others. For example, you may be a hard-working and conscientious employee, but if you go to a job interview with your body covered in tattoos, your hair dyed strange colors and cut in an extreme and outlandish manner, you have various piercings, and you just have a general look of unkemptness and oddness—you probably can tell how your potential boss would react. You may be very respectful and carry on a good conversation, but your chosen appearance casts a shadow of doubt upon your character.

In the same way, you may look and dress fine for an occasion, but a lack of eye contact and manners could be a problem. Also, we may look respectable and speak well, but if we convey an attitude of over-confidence and inconsiderateness, that could also be a problem. This doesn't just apply to job interviews, in fact, most employers don't care how kindhearted their employees are as long as they do good work. This really applies better to familial relationships and friendships. If you don't know how to be appealing, you will make fewer friends, what friendships you do have will not be as close, and some friendships may be lost because of our unsavory personality. As I mentioned in chapter 4, having a good sense of humor is the primary quality that makes people approachable. You may be kind, but if you are stern, stoic, and unsmiling, people will not likely choose to befriend you. On the other hand, if you can take life a little lighter and see the humor in things, you will make people feel comfortable. That's not to say you should be a jokester either; then, when a serious subject arises, a friend would avoid confiding in you. It's a delicate balance. If you are a clown, try toning it down. Hey! That's a funny phrase to remember: "If you're a clown, tone it down." There's an example of humor, I just amused myself with that rhyme.

On the other hand, if you have trouble finding humor in life, follow this protocol. I'm not a trained doctor, but I identify as a doctor, so that makes me a doctor. As your humor doctor, I'm going to write you a prescription: read Tom Sawyer by Mark Twain. I guarantee you, my friend, you'll be busting open your sides from laughing, and if you don't learn a sense of humor from that, nothing will. If Tom Sawyer doesn't make you laugh, then you might have a serious health condition: Nolaughingitis, and you'll definitely need a better doctor than me, perhaps a psychologist. Putting my jokes aside, I sincerely hope that even if you already have a good sense of humor, Tom Sawyer will make it even better. It's hilarious, I assure you. Have you ever heard the saying: "Laughing is the best medicine"? It certainly is, just laughing, even when it's fake, makes you feel much better. It's what makes life most memorable and enjoyable.

Try it now, if there's nobody around to hear you, or even if there are people and you just don't care—try faking laughter. It works, it comes naturally, at least for me, just thinking about laughing makes me giggle, it's contagious like yawning. It's plenty of fun, it's a medicine that spreads to others, making your life more pleasant, and the same for those around you. Being kind, humble, and having a good sense of humor alone will make people excuse most mistakes of yours because you will be so pleasant to be around.

I know I said being pleasant to be around is not about physical beauty, but nonetheless, I'd like to give you a few simple tips on that subject while I'm on it. So, you would be wise to wash your face, smile, brush your teeth, wear clothes that look nice (if you're with city people; in the country, most folks don't care if you look like you just came out of a mudwallow), fix your hair decently, and so forth. Not to be rude, but if others smell objectionable odors only in your presence, they may feel the need to increase the distance between the two of you. If you have been chewing tobacco or eating chocolate, a good brushing might do the trick. Also, stand in a good posture, don't slump over. If you slouch, you'll look bored, uninterested, sad, tired, sickly, etc. I would recommend against strong perfumes and colognes because they can be overpowering and distracting. I would also recommend against wearing jeans that look like they've been mauled by a panther (ripped jeans). My work jeans get ripped from hard work, but then I sew them back together. Of course, everybody is entitled to their own opinion, but in my opinion, it seems silly to purposefully buy jeans that are ruined before you even use them; leave it to modern fashion to convince people to wear and do odd things! Heavy makeup is also distracting and extreme-looking. Everything in moderation.

Also, if you like people, don't be afraid to show it. This is not just about romantic interest, it also applies equally to friends, young or old. If you feel you've found a "kindred-spirit," then seek to further that friendship. Old people generally enjoy the company of young people, but many young people only want to be around those of their own age. I understand that, it's only natural that we should be drawn to people at a similar stage in life. And, of course, if you want to go backpacking in the wilderness, old granny may not be the companion you're looking for. But I believe that each of us is enriched by a variety of companions. Those of the other sex, younger folks, older folks, people of all backgrounds and upbringings. Now, I won't lie, being from the country myself, I can tolerate the company of city people only so long before I yearn to be among my own kind again. But, every once in a while, it may be nice to shake things up a bit, to meet strange people. It's only by chance/coincidence, destiny/fate, or searching/scouring that you'll find the right people for you; or maybe you already have them right now, right at home, you've known them since birth— your family.

Oftentimes we have to lose something before you can truly appreciate it. You may have to leave your family, your homeland, your culture, maybe even your beliefs for a while, in order to realize that the treasure you sought was at home all along. Or maybe you were born for a different way of life, it's up to you to find out. Don't content yourself with reading books and watching movies about adventure, do it yourself! Go on your own journey.

In Europe, it is common practice for young people just-graduated, to go on an adventure before they commit to college or a job, to satisfy that fundamental urge to wander freely—it is called a Gap Year. In America, unfortunately, this is very uncommon. Most graduates immediately go on to a job, college, or just do nothing and mooch off their parents. What if we made a Gap Year a tradition in America? Wouldn't that enrich our young people? In Europe, the working hours are lower, and vacation days are more numerous. In America, we, on average, work longer than the average Medieval serf, and I am serious about this.

How long will you spend your life not doing the things you love, doing the same thing over and over and over again, running the rat race round and round the hamster wheel day after day? How long will you keep wishing it isn't Monday, then wish it was the weekend, then wish it was a vacation, then wish you were retired? Let me give you the answer to those questions, let me tell you what'll happen if you don't know yet: pretty soon, you'll wish your whole life away. It is strange how it's generally older folks that end up living their dreams (albeit probably not as they imagined because they are not quite as spry as they used to be), while the young, wild, adventurous kids force themselves to study and labor. There is still plenty of mystery and adventure left in the world, it's up to you to find it. Once again, I'll recommend to you The Alchemist by Paulo Coelho because it does a perfect, wonderfully entertaining, enlightening job of showing what I just said. It is an allegorical tale about a young Spanish shepherd boy from Andalusia who has a dream about a treasure, which leads him on a marvelous journey across the Sahara desert of North Africa. It is a wonderful book, and to be honest, far better than this one!

I was once asked in school: "What is freedom?" Everybody sees freedom as something a little different. Sometimes our ideas about freedom might interfere with the freedoms of others. Consider this: to you, what is freedom? It might take a little while to figure it out and find the right words to express it. To me, put simply, freedom is the ability to reach my full potential in life, to accomplish my purpose in life, to be a seeker of truth. That doesn't interfere with the freedoms of others, now, does it? In fact, I hope to use my freedom to help many people.

If you know what freedom is to you, you will know whether or not you are achieving that freedom. You may realize that, according to your definition of freedom, you may not currently be free, you might be in prison. If so, then figure out how to become free. I say this so that you will be content and at peace with yourself, with life, and with others. If you are trapped in a cage, like a poor bird, yearning to fly free, you will beat your wings against the metal bars until they're bloody, peck the cage until your beak breaks. If you do that, you will be unhappy and everyone around you will sense it and suffer; eventually, they will grow tired of being with a person who lashes out at them because you are not free and yearn to be free.

To have good friends, not "friends" that you make with the tap of a button on social media, nor just acquaintances, nor just even people you "hang out" with, no, I want you to have lifelong companions that stand by you through thick and thin. Have you ever heard the country song, Find Out Who Your Friends Are? In it, the lyrics say: "Get yourself in a bind...you find out who your friends are, somebody's gonna drop everything, run out and crank up their car, hit the gas, get there fast, never stop to think 'what's in it for me' or 'it's way too far,' they just show on up, with a big old heart." I pray that such friends may be your companions through life, and that you likewise help them through the trials and tribulations of life, and that you have or find your foremost friend on earth, your spouse.

In Chapter 5: Understanding Psychology, we dove into the subject of how humans think, how you and I think, how our ways of thinking affect our lives, and what we can do to change our thinking to go in a better direction. As usual, the next step is to put it to practice.

The foremost thing I want you to get out of this chapter, and this whole book, is that we are all interconnected, that we do better together. The best way to make life easy, make friends, be self-sufficient, and be connected with nature is to make a community of like-minded people. You don't have to join some commune or start one, in your own neighborhood you could start this on a small scale. Help your neighbors out, not asking for anything in return. Do errands, mow the grass, shovel the snow, and whatnot.

If you start doing "good turns" without being paid, your neighbors will likewise feel the need to help you out when you need them. Paying people for a service settles the debt, so that no one needs to feel beholden or indebted to another person. But if we would create a system of helping each other without expectation of reward, recompense, or payment, we will create a better neighborhood and better people therein. If you have some junk, "one man's junk is another man's treasure," ask around and see who needs it or put it outside with a "Free" sign on it. Share your tools with your neighbors, give them gifts, talk to them, have them over for dinner or a game of some sort, have a block party, have a community garden, and the list of endless possibilities goes on and on.

Extend your community beyond the bounds of mankind. Get to know the forest around your place, get to know the plants and animals. I know each and every tree where I grew up, every hummingbird, every lizard, every frog, and every hill and hole. Learn the wild plants in your area, wherever you may be, I guarantee you that you have a veritable garden growing wild somewhere nearby. Knowing the plants gives you plenty of good things to eat for free, it immerses you in your landscape, and makes you happier. Here are a few resources: get the book Peterson Field Guide to Edible Wild Plants, if you have a device, download the app Plantnet, which will help you accurately identify your local plants with more certainty than a book can. Go on local foraging walks (do some research to find one in your area), check out the outdoorsman, Rob Greenfield's site https://www.robgreenfield.org/findaforager/ to find a good forager near you. Mr. Greenfield also has a YouTube channel called by his name, which I encourage you to check out for its numerous useful tips.

Of course, many people would not like this, but I just want to give you some pointers. If you want, learn how to hunt and fish, if you don't already know how. With regards to fishing, figure out what would work best in your area, whether it be surf fishing, creek fishing, lake fishing, river fishing, fly fishing, or whatever else. Learn the techniques and get the appropriate equipment. With regards to hunting, find a suitable firearm, or if you would prefer, a bow or crossbow. Learn how to use it safely, take a hunter's education course, get a license, and find some good spots in your area. I understand you may despise the thought of killing an animal, but it could give you a way of getting cheap food when things get too expensive, especially if you don't yet have a farm. Also, relying on nature as your source of livelihood, even if only in a small way (just for fun), it makes you feel more whole and fulfilled.

Here's a good example of neighborliness: one of my relatives, who lives in a Latino neighborhood, would see goats wandering around and grazing on people's yards. What did he do? Call animal control? Call the sheriff? Some of my neighbors have unfortunately done that. No, he thought nothing of it, he just enjoyed watching them. His neighbors, who at the time didn't know him, invited him to a block party. They slaughtered one of their goats, made all kinds of Mexican cuisine, and played mariachi music. By the end of it, he was good friends with all his neighbors. If you have a problem with what your neighbors are doing, don't go to the police, go to them! Honestly, that is the act of a coward to hide inside the house and call the authorities on your own neighbor. But, nowadays, in this modern world, being a neighbor doesn't really mean much. Most people have never met them, or even if they have met them they hardly know them. People love to be independent and private, so be it, that's their choice. Life is easier and happier with a broad community to support you, "many hands make the load light."

Create a close-knit tribe, and don't limit it only to your blood relatives. I once saw a doormat that said: "Friends are your chosen family." Please do not keep friends at arms' length, don't hold them back, don't shut them out. Right now, it seems to be a choice to be neighborly or not, but in the future, we may be forced to rely on each other. When times get hard, which may not be as far off as you think, the people you'll need will not be your family across the country, across the state, or even across the town— they'll be your neighbors across the street. Grow a good relationship with them now to make it easier when things get hard. Out West in the USA, during the frontier period, gunslingers and "hired guns" would say: "there's only the fast and the dead." No in-betweens. If you do not know, this is referring to a gunman's quickness to the draw.

We may not be engaging in duels in the future, but we probably will be engaging in a scramble to survive. We see it every time a hurricane comes: people rush to the stores, empty the shelves, and stock up; same thing happens when there's some kind of shortage, people will literally fight each other to get a tank of gas. Most people's "civilized" nature disappears when civilization disappears; and what ensues? Violence, brutality, injustice, barbarism, selfishness, destruction, sickness, and death. I want you to have the advantage when that dreaded day comes, I want you to draw your gun even before the gunfight, I want you to survive. This is not just grim theorization, our society, inch by inch, little by little, descends into disaster. Our modern, technological lifestyle is inherently negative and destructive to our minds, bodies, and the land. It will inevitably catch up to us at some point, in one way or another. It may not be in your lifetime, but then, prepare your children for whatever comes, make them strong, tough, kind, and good. Teach them honesty, give them a community wherein to play outside and make friends, to dig holes, and climb trees. Give them a future and a hope. May it not be, that our desperation to make money and move up the ladder—may it not be that these things deprive our children from their inheritance: a world of plentiful nature and freedom.

To be completely honest, this all seems overly complicated to me, I wish the world was simpler. In a simpler world, you wouldn't have to spend your hard-earned money on a book about making friends, you'd just have friends! But this is a choice, we can choose to simplify our lives. All I ask of you is that you work hard to find a way of creating a healthy, wholesome, natural, and harmonious environment for yourself, your family, and those around you who you are able to help. My goal is for you to not need this book. My goal is for you to burn this confounded book! When you're ready, just embrace your destruction tendencies and set this book afire. You won't need it any more.

As a parting request before you put down this book, if you found this book useful, then we would be much obliged if you would write a review on Amazon and share it with your friends and family to help them on their journey as well. I hope I helped you in some little way. There's much more to do out there, plenty of mystery, frontier, and adventure left for the taking—chase after it!

In all that you do, I wish you only the very best.

How To Change Your Mindset and Rewire Your Brain

Christopher Rothchester

Introduction

Have you ever wanted to change who you are, like a moth to a butterfly? Well, that starts by rewriting your mind through methodical steps. The million-dollar word to consider is: Neuroplasticity. What that big college exam word means, is the ability of your brain to re-energize synaptic connections through learning. The root word, Neuro, is derived from the words 'Nervous System.' Plasticity comes from 'plastos', a Greek word for moldable. Hence, the nervous system has a moldable brain and Neuroplasticity. It's to create connections and pathways between neurons. This highfalutin term was introduced by Polish neuroscientist Jerzy Konorski not long before the Titanic sank in 1906. As a writer who has experienced symptoms of anxiety overthinking and was once tested to have ADHD, these are some awesome tips and tricks to help remedy some of those situations.

First, let's learn a bit about the brain. Within the brain are 100 billion neurons. It's only in the last 10 years did medical scientists learn that the brain grows well into the adult years. So the question is, how can you grow your brain through neuroplasticity? It all starts with the hippocampus, the memory cortex part of the brain. Twenty years ago, there was evidence that listening to Mozart's Sonata can increase one's IQ. So in the state of Georgia, everybody born was given a Mozart album to listen to in Georgia. The result: no change in IQ. What that is called, according to neuroscientist Richard Haier, is the schmozart effect. Meaning: it has been thoroughly debunked as quackery. What you can do, is the little thing in this book to develop your brain. The question is, can an old dog be taught new tricks? Short answer: Yes.

In the 1890s psychologist, William James theorized that the brain is not changing into adulthood. It's fixed. He wrote that organic matter has a tough degree of plasticity which means, he thought, one can't change much once they reach adulthood. Just like the above Mozart album, that trend was debunked in modern times. Decades later, in the 1920s Karl Lashley, a researcher found that neural pathways within Rhesus Monkeys—a break thought was formed in science in the understanding of the changes in the brain and Neuroplasticity. Then in 1960, a team of researchers studied people who had strokes and then were able to regain the usage of a limb again like magic. Which revealed a new fact: the brain grows and is malleable into adulthood and can rewire itself to learn.

There is a lot of medical and scientific information here, and chances are—well—you're not a doctor. But in layman's terms, it is documented that most neurodegenerative diseases harken from degenerative loss of neuroplasticity. Some of the usual suspects with mental illness are tied to that tweaking, such as Alzheimer's disease, Parkinson's disease, and Huntington's disease. This guide will give a step-by-step approach to how you can improve your brain through a series of techniques. From learning about turning a negative into a positive to a little thing called emotional intelligence. So let's begin our adventure into consciousness growth or mindset shift.

Or... maybe helps you get a bit better at Wordle.

Chapter 1: Using Neuroplasticity to Success

First things first, neuroplasticity is the strengthening of neuronal pathways in your brain. This book will avoid using platitudes and attempt to get into the nitty-gritty of how to improve your brain. Let's start at the beginning. At birth, a baby has 2,500 synapses, but by age three, there are 15,000. These tiny things in the brain are tiny gaps in between neurons where the nerve impulses system communicates. By using various techniques, it improves your mind's malleability so you can retain more info and be more efficient at doing it. This is called synaptic plasticity. This is the ability of your networks in your brain to reorganize through new information and rewire differently than it was before, so you are more adaptable to doing it.

Example: You never studied the topic of the ancient Rome colosseum, and then you gotta do a book report on it, and then talk about it fluently? Then will help one expand the plastic in their brain. Doing Out Of Comfort Zone things, again and again can improve cognitive functions and improve your ability to learn and even get better at your day job. One wants a malleability brain that can adapt to new things on the fly and not be settled by the same repetitive behavior.

The conscious and subconscious work hand and hand, according to Sigmund Freud. According to recent research, 'rewriting' your brain can have huge changes in your life and can spearhead improvement. So what does that word mean exactly? Well, it's using science to my shrewd and repetitive new patterns to create positive results. Thanks to the understanding of science and Brain chemistry, when you were once 'set in your ways,' you can become anew. Gradually, though embedding that pattern into your subconscious, it becomes second nature. According to

Michael Merzenich, who is a renowned neuroscientist at the University of California, your mind likes to filter what it can remember and then ignore stuff it doesn't want to remember, and one should refocus attention on their goals.

One does not need to do aggressive mental gymnastics like astrophysics or trigonometry to grow their brain. Just thought-provoking repetition in a positive manner. A person's unconscious also develops neurons by doing tasks to stimulate the mind. Day by day, if you continue to work at something and strive to be better at it, it will one day slowly change your life like a metamorphosis to a butterfly. The two main definitions of neuroplasticity:

1.1 Functional Plasticity

This first one isn't related to just 'getting smarter' but is more actually related to damage. When a brain is damaged, maybe by accident, and can rewire that part of the brain to a new one. When you once couldn't move your right hand due to a terrible collision through therapy, perhaps you'll be able to move that hand again.

Structural plasticity This is when the brain can change its structure through malleability by simply learning. When your brain is dominant in one area, through repetition and hard work, your brain structure can change through hard work. Couldn't play the violin? Maybe, a few months from now, you can go through that little thing called Structural Plasticity.

Some of the things that can happen when you are knowable with Neuroplasticity:

- Learn new things and retain that information

- Become even better as current skills by enhancing cognitive skills
- If having a stroke or traumatic brain energy, one can recover quicker
- Improves areas in the brain that are slowing down through the passage of time and/or fight against developing Alzheimer's
- Using Improvements that can boost your mental agility and brain fitness

With the more complex terminology out of the way, let's get more to common tongue nonmedical language.

First, let's learn a bit about the different types of neuroplasticity so you can, well, get smarter and grow your brain even more. The first is functional plasticity, the mind's ability to move if there is a damaged area in the brain or other areas that aren't hurt. On the other hand, structural plasticity is the brain's structure and acute changes from the ability to learn. The most important part of this book is the ability to learn. What that does is improves your Brain-Derived Neurotrophic Factor. A child's brain develops neurons at an astonishing rate up until three; learning about it can help develop your mind for the betterment of yourself. Using this technique will help you overcome or (being honest) lessen the symptoms of panic, anxiety, depression, overthinking, and ADHD. Within some of the following tips, you learn how to rewire your brain to just retain more information and be more apt to get out of your comfort zone and… live a little more boldly by using the little thing called Neuroplasticity.

There are many things one can do to improve your neuroplasticity, but here are seven of them. For example, you, in theory, can be a total introvert and then be an extrovert by simple brain plasticity enhancements. Diametrically the opposite, From one extreme to the other. A real-life example of that would be tongue-wagging free-throw dunking former NBA Superstar Michael Jordan. Who, while playing basketball in North Carolina, had an Achilles Heel, the main weakness in his game. That was: he couldn't dribble well, according to Teammate Kenny "The Jet" Smith would then say was dribbling. Well, the next time he saw him, he became a vastly better ball handler where that weakness in his game could not be exploited. "The only guy whose weaknesses became his strengths." That is a prime example of physically getting better at something, dribbing, but the same rules apply to mentally getting better too.

Without further ado, here are some tips to light millions of pathways up in your brain.

1.2 Steps How To Improve Neuroplasticity

1. Mental Gymnastics - Challenge yourself. Whatever you want to do in life, maybe it is being an astrophysicist, learning to be a gardener, doing something that challenges you, and working at it and thinking about it—often. It doesn't have to be anything big or daring, but something out of your comfort zone. Depending on your age, maybe start doing things accessible and easy and work your way up. But do something that is thought-provoking. Crossword puzzles change to, but so does complex writing on things like neuroplasticity, for instance. What you want to do and look at your Achilles' heel or your general weakness, use grit and determination to strive to be better at that. There are studies that highly successful people put forth 15 to 30 minutes a day to just--think and assess new information that they got. What that little bit of time does is helps you plot your next move like a game of

chess. But some of the time, there are more scientifically proven things to improve your brain.

2. Running

According to the Epidemiological evidence from the National Library of Medicine, exercise improves Neuroplasticity and helps ward off Alzheimer's Disease.

Whenever your blood is pumping in aerobic activities, you can increase the Neuroplasticity in your brain. What this does is it will improve your cognitive and motor function in your brain so you can expand your horizons and get that much better at things. This is also said to help best, hippocampus for memory and learning. The other silver lining of this: you could help ward off dementia. Simply sprinting can boost your Brain-derived neurotrophic factor, AKA BDNF, which is a key molecule in the plastic altercations in the brain. Things like memory and learning are tied to this. Some good exercises are running but also weight lifting, aggressive sports, and dancing, but the more physical heart-pumping exhausting, the better... like sprinting. Other things exercise does for cardiovascular health is, Lower blood pressure, Help regulate blood sugar, Reduce asthma symptoms, Reduce chronic pain, Aids sleep, Regulates weight, Strengthen the immune system, boost mode, reduces risks of falls, and last but not least Improve brain power for Neuroplasticity.

3. Make Art

From research in 2015, it was found whenever you do art; there is a positive behavior change in the brain. Frontal white matter is reorganized whenever you do something artistic. You don't have to be Michelangelo's creating the Sistine Chapel to consider yourself an artist. Start doing basic things, basic noodles, writing projects, or paintings and you can both improve your outlook on life but also help neuroplasticity in your brain. Painting, for instance, improves Cortical and cerebellar activity whenever you get better at drawing. Doing art doesn't just improve your brain; it helps you self problems, reduces depression, and helps with relaxation. You are just limited to visual art, creating music also has been proven to promote neuroplasticity. According to research, it improves memory, prevention, and motor skills and causes the age-related decline of the brain. In the day and age of the internet, there are tons of ways to learn how to compose music, paint, and draw. The first destination for people on a budget and limited time: Youtube. Another idea: apps. For learning to play guitar, the gold standard app is Yousician.

4. Learn a Second Language

According to the National Library of Medicine study, learning a second language can have positive changes in White-Matter Connectivity. It brings greater strength to the brain's connectivity between regions in the brain. You can learn a new language at any age to help improve your mental acuity, vocabulary, ability to multi-task, and creativity skills. Many apps can make learning a new language, well, not exactly easy, but the easiest it's ever been. Duolingo is an app from all stores that makes learning Spanish with childlike simplicity and colorful graphics. But it's about being persistent and determined to retain the info and keep at it, it is what will make you truly get positive Morphological brain changes.

5. Read and Learn Everyday

The United States is ranked 125th on the global literacy ranking. There are many states where the budget is distractedly different for adult education to get people to learn. In this competitive world, reading, and reading every day on your passion topic can be a deciding factor in your growth. Not only reading but make a calculate an effort to learn every day and open-minded to things that you may not initially be excited by but through an open mind, this becomes more interesting to you. Many of the chapters give information on how to retain new info, sleeping, exercise, the eating right, but one has to have an unbridled passion for learning every day. One has to be in a frame of mind of continuous learning. Also, not just in familiar topics, too. If your weakness is not knowing ___ then study up on ___ until you are adept.

6. Sleep

This is consistent with one-third of a person's life and is critical to brain plasticity—-among other things. As everybody with half a brain knows, a healthy amount of z's is essential for energy restoration and also your immune system. If you want to learn how to play the violin, instead of putting in long hours and cutting your sleep back, make sure you get your proper 7-9 hours of sleep. Things to watch for: make sure you get the proper REM sleep, and this can roughly be tabulated by Smart Watch. Various studies prove just how vital sleep is to not your brain but also your entire body. TED conference on Youtube with a professor of neuroscience/psychology Matt Walker. During it, he gives hard truths about how critical sleep is. Including health, retaining info & creativity.

7. Meditation

Magnetoencephalography Studies that there is a correlation between meditation and neural plasticity. Another thing that can be done is using simple Vipassanā, the Indian word for 'insight,' using meditation. There are many types of meditation, and they consist of mindfulness meditation, from spiritual meditation to focused meditation movement. Both the easiest ones for starter meditators would be mindful meditation and spiritual meditation (prayer). For the former, one just has to close their eyes, remain still, and have pleasant and empty thoughts go into your head. Stuff like focusing on the quietness of there or your own heartbeat. That drowns out energy-draining, overzealous thoughts and helps both reduce anxiety and help ward off Alzheimer's and depression, but at the same token, breath boosts your brain's ability to learn. The first thing to learn with meditation is simple breathing exercises like Diaphragmatic breathing. The first: is the 4-7-8 breathing technique.

8. Ketosis (Fat), DHA (Found In Fish Oils)

This is a high-fat diet contestant with low carbs. It's used to control epilepsy in children, but more than that. Typically, the brain uses glucose from carbohydrates for energy in the body. But when you avoid eating those foods and start fasting, the body enters into the fat and is broken down into what is called ketosis. The body starts using fatty acids from a molecule named Beta-Hydroxybutyrate. What this does is improves Long-Term Potentiation (meaning, increase the strength of nerve impulses along pathways). Essentially, subscribing to the Mediterranean diet and basically eating healthier, and getting more omega-3 found in fish royal into your system, can help you learn. Studies say that Omega-3, a fatty acid found in fish, can improve neurogenesis. Eating a good amount of this can help your brain development and muscle activity and also cell growth. According to the National Library of Medicine, it helps develop synaptic plasticity in the brain. There are other benefits of heating seafood: it prevents cell death from antiapoptotic effects and the imbalance of free radicals and antioxidants within one's system, called anti-oxidative stress, and helps reduce inflammation. In Layman's terms: it does a lot for the mind and the body.

9. Magnesium

As noted, instead of your key ingredients to help your brain from some scratchy wonder pill from Dr. Oz, get it from eating leafy foods. Studies say that a healthy amount of maximum improves the visual cortex in mice. It is also tied to hundreds of biochemical reactions in your body, like anti-inflammatory benefits and cognitive function. This is part of a critical physiological role in the development of the brain. Again, it is best to eat food like vegetables, dark green in color, grains, milk, and yogurt instead of popping a wonder pill.

10. Reduce Stress

Neurogenesis has found some startling facts: Chronic stress can hinder the neuronal adoption needed to improve your brain. This form of stress causes neurons in the brain to change, either shrink or grow. It reduces the hippocampus and prefrontal cortex's ability to have positive neuroplasticity. Furthermore, chronic stress can alter spine destiny and dendritic length, and this branches into the prefrontal cortex. So if you are a person that gets proper sleep, with no substance abuse problems, exercises, and still has a hard time remembering... it might be because your brain is in a fight or flight response from stress. So if you have a high-stress job, which many people do, meditation or a midday jog to help reduce the stress and improve the circuitry of the brain.

11. Fast

Intermittent fasting is documented to improve brain cognitive performance, according to the National Library of Medicine. What it does is it helps increase the Brain-derived neurotrophic factor (BDNF) and, from some estimates online, by 50% to 400%. According to Mark Mattson at the National Institute on Aging, it can delay Parkinson's and Alzheimer's. However, starving yourself for long periods has the opposite effect. The key words are intermittent fasting. Mattson argues that our genes are from our ancestors who did have 3 square meals a day plus a nice snack. Rather, our bodies were built to go into occasional fasting mode, and our brain reacts accordingly.

12. Travel

One doesn't need to go to Bangladesh to consider that traveling either. It is all about going out of your comfort zone. Consider venturing on a troll to a nice safe area you never walk to, going shopping somewhere else, or simply going on a hike. Studies say that traveling can boost your BDNF levels and your cognitive flexibility. The reason: you are out of your element, and your brain is forced to create new synapses faster. There also is what is called Virtual Travel, where you can see different places on YouTube if you are really walking there. Essentially, to improve your brain, you should avoid following the beaten path every day that does not develop your brain and broaden your way of thinking.

13. Eating Right/Turmeric Curcumin

According to the National Library of Medicine, this orange-in-color spice can to wonders for your Hippocampal Circuits and Attenuates. This Ayurvedic medicine has been used for centuries in Middle Eastern and Asian countries. A study was conducted on rats with depression, and this powder helped reduce symptoms of it. Also, Curcumin Alters Neural Plasticity for the improvement of the brain. During clinical trials testing people with MDD, Major Depressive Disorder/ Curcumin can help reduce it. But it certainly wouldn't hurt to try to improve our brain using these. However, if you really want to improve your brain, you have to do a variety of things and not just put spice in your food. The other more simple thing to do is just eat better sustenance. Best example: is the Mediterranean diet. Filled with fish, nuts, bread, fruits, vegetables, and little red meats or artery-clogging gut-busting processed food.

1.2 Summary

This is a variety of medically proven ways to improve the plasticity of your brain. To help slow down cognitive decline, the sooner you practice better brain health, the more likely you will have a fresher brain as you get older. According to the Alzheimer's Association, Age, family history, genetics, and other factors like an injury to the head or healthy aging. But formulating a strategy to now just improve your brain for job performance but to avoid certain degenerate diseases is vital to your health.

Chapter 2: A Winner's Belief System

Tom Brady is widely considered the greatest football player of all time. He has a whopping seven Super Bowl rings and is still playing as a starting QB into his 40s. Even if you negate the seven Super Bowls, that is still quite the accomplishment to still be playing. He had trust in the system with Bill Belichick and, afterward, Bruce Arians. What he has is a quintessential winner's belief system. A mindset to overcome adversity and become the best at his profession. If you are looking to pattern yourself off of a winner's mentality—-it starts with good building blocks and a positive attitude. Have a powerful belief system within yourself, unshakable, unbreakable, and incorruptible, and you will be on a pathway to significant self-improvement. There are ways that if you visualize an ideal version of yourself, maybe years from now, and then start to just walk, talk and act like that person... you will eventually become that person. A winner's mindset like Tom Brady's stems from an innermost belief in one's self, the system he worked in, and steady improvement and listening to constructive feedback. The reason is what you think dictates our behavior. Here are some points of self-improve that could fundamentally change who you are for your own welfare. But the best thing that could help: check your ego at the door.

2.1 Steps How To Develop a Winner's Belief System

Growth Mindset - Having the mental state that your brain is a sapling looking to grow as tall as a 250-foot ancient tree that is a couple of thousand years old tree called General Sherman. Meaning there is a ton of growing one can do even when reaching adulthood. Your mind needs to grow, and if you already think you are great and something, chances are that you will have a harder time getting even better. Writers, in particular, at a young age want to think they are the next Stephen King, and they push away all negative feedback because they have made up their minds. What they have done has put them in a fixed mindset that hinders their growth potential. Always stay in a young sapling frame of mind.

2. Get Out Of Your Comfort Zone

Following the same repetitious path is not going to develop you develop your skills. Learn to get out of your usual parameters. Just like with weight lifting, where if you do the same workout, the muscle memory learns, and then it's harder to make gains. If you start doing other workouts to work for different muscle groups, just like the mind, you can grow again. Tackle Fear and uncertainty of newness as a way to live life. Go into uncharted waters (not dangerous ones, of course. No rock climbing without a harness, for instance). Think of new adventures as a way to live life and not fear. The aforementioned Tom Brady did the exact same thing when he went from New England to Tampa Bay. In the wise words of Morgan Freeman in The Shawshank Redemption, "Get busy living or get busy dying."

3. Formulate a Winning Strategy

Simply mapping out in your mind, or maybe in a journal, a way to achieve your goal to be an astronaut, or whatever, is your first step to actually being one. Formulate something through preparation and mental fortitude. Whatever your dreams may be, having a strategy for the way to get them is the pathway. Research the winning strategies in your field. Perhaps, duplicate the same methodology of someone else. Improvise. Or, if you're using anything involving technology, embrace the latest forms of technology and the Internet. Also, sometimes (usually) some things may take longer than expected. If one has a winning strategy, it may take time, but perseverance is your greatest ally. Be your own Bill Belichick.

4. Have a Contingency Plan

On the flip side of the strategy, the more pessimistic side, make sure and have at least some form of contingency plan in case things do not go exactly according to plan. Sometimes plan B can open the doors to plan A. This next part does contradict the idea of having a positive outlook, but it's still good to be prepared in case something does happen . There is this thing called Murphy's Law. The first rule is, Anything that can go wrong will go wrong. The second rule: Nothing is as easy as it looks (also pessimist). Finally, the third rule is: Everything takes longer than you think it will. Though all of these are pessimistic attitudes, it's always good to have at least some type of backup plan in case the worst does happen.

5. Seek to Be an Expert

One has to be realistic, but one can be an expert in many fields when one puts forth maximum effort and grit. It is nature versus nurture. The age-old question... or both? For some professionals, there is a ton of nature, meaning you're born with many skills or physical attributes that help you do this job better. But on the other side of the coin, there is a nurturer where if you do enough of a certain professional in the off hours and put forth perhaps thousands of hours into it, get a degree; you may become an expert. The major * on this segment: artistic endeavors and sports careers are extraordinarily difficult to become an expert at. Those two professions are a healthy dose of born with it nature versus standard nurture professionals like becoming a volleyball coach. Whatever your dreams may be, go for it.

6. Focus, Focus, Focus, Focus

In the day and age of TikTok, crying kids, apocalyptic politics, and tons of streaming content, there are innumerable ways to be distracted from your endeavors. But the difference between someone who can achieve their goals and not: is a razor-sharp focus. Eliminate distractions and have a 'me time' where you can focus on your lofty ambitions each and every day... preferably at the same time every day, creating a habit. For instance, most writers, in particular, create an iron-clad routine where they write every day at the same time. Stephen King, for instance, writes the same 2000 words every day, 7 days a week. I'm not saying you have to have a Herculean work ethic, but if you just have to focus on that bull's eye every day, step a little closer each day... you got a leg up on your competition.

7. Embrace Change

Bob Dylan has a song The Times Are A-Changin'. Truth be told, time is always in flux, so one has to learn to adapt to change. Another quote, "The One Most Adaptable to Change is the One that Survives." By Charles Darwin. Embrace change and handle it in stride. Not only that, realize without a little change from the beaten path, things can be a little dull. As noted in the neuroplasticity chapter above, embracing change isn't just a winning mindset; it's a way to prove your mental acuity. So instead of being habitual with a thing like you are under mental enslavement, realize you have free thought to do whatever you like (legally) in order to grow your mind and, in a competitive spirit, be a winner.

8. Don't Be a Sore Loser

If you've heard the expression before, to know how to win, one must know how to lose... and sometimes many times. If you lose too graciously, and not just in sports, but have setbacks in life, do not lose motivation. The Iconic politician Winston Churchill had a quote on this, "Success consists of going from failure to failure without loss of enthusiasm." Elon Musk's SpaceX had 3 rockets that failed before its fourth one launched and was the first privately-developed rocket in orbit. If first, you don't succeed, try, try, again through practice and determination. One of the positive things about losing is giving you a second chance at it using all the knowledge you acquired to try it again and again. If one keeps proper tenacity even when they get a bad deck of cards, they may be able to win the race through sheer willpower. So when you redouble your effort, renew your strategy, and spearhead forth with confidence and might, you might see just the W the next time.

9. Be Flexible and Calm to Change Strategy on the Fly

This is a microcosm of what you can do on the fly with your chips down. Michael Jordan was losing with seconds to go in the 1998 NBA finals he kept his composure. The score was 85-86, Jazz with the lead with 37.1 seconds left. The crowd in Salt Lake City was on their feet, cheering and on pins and needles of suspense. What Jordan did, as John Stocking passed the ball to Karl Malone Jordan recognized they were running the same play in the paint in the lost post. So Jordan remembered that, with catlike agility, he came to Malone's blindside and stole the ball from him like a bandit and dibbled out the court with calm. With seconds to spare, Bulls coach Phil Jackson did not do a time so the Jazz could not set up the defense. His Airness the ball and slowly dribbled up the court to each up the most time on the clock. With the clock ticking down, Michael did a cross-over on Bryan Russell and the topic of the free-throw line and shot the ball. Swish. Only 5.2 seconds remained and used his mental fortitude and made the game-winning shot. The most famous shot in NBA history was made. All of this is a strategy for how you can completely change your strategy to win as long as you keep your composure and mind open for the winning game plan.

10 . Competition Is a Good Thing

Speaking about competition, if you have somebody who can inspire you in some fourth of competition, be it a writing partner, fellow salesman, or maybe a salon owner, you can use competitors to reach an even higher echelon. Competition is a good thing. If you are a person who wants to be a master in some type of field—-or maybe even competent, have somebody who can play off to maximize your performance. A good example would be Bulls player Scottie Pippen got to play with Michael Jordan. They practiced together. And went against one another in scrimmages. Though MJ is generally considered the GOAT, the greatest player of all time, he also helped Scottie Pippen reach the zenith of his potential by working with MJ and seeing the dedication, work ethic, and, most of all competitive spirit he brought forth in every game So if you are a rookie in your field, or an intermediate, look to that top dog in the field to inspire you to use as a competitor motivator. It may not happen overnight, or maybe never, but the competition will make you better at your craft than if you were left in solitude. Anybody you can feed off of can help you strive for your best.

11. Find a Winning Team

"Great teamwork is the only way we create the breakthroughs that define our careers." - Pat Riley. If you don't have a team, or at least some type of person, that can coalesce around, it is going to be challenging to reach your pinnacle. Depending on your career, writing, for instance, which is a job of solitude (usually), you still do indeed need some time of 'team' to reach the furthest potential (an editor, publisher). If you indeed rise up to the ranks in your very lone wolf professional—-at the end of the day, you will be in a team. Because even a lone-wolf job or personality needs constructive feedback from a team to reach that apex. Francis Ford Coppola wrote the screenplay for The Godfather, but he also collaborated with Mario Puzo. Then he worked within a team to find the best people and hired Al Pacino and Marlon Brando. WW2 mathematician Alan Turing worked with a team to break the Nazis' U-Boat Enigma. All jobs, solo jobs, and team jobs, eventually lead to teamwork and interpersonal skills. So whatever professional there is you yearn for, learning to work within a team is crucial to the macrocosm of things.

12. Research the Best

The Baddest Man on the Plant, Mike Tyson, was idolized by Muhammad Ali. Oprah Winfrey said her inspiration was Maya Angelou. Steve Jobs saw Polaroid entrepreneur Edwin Land as his hero. Whatever your modus operandi is with your career and your life, find a beacon of light to strive for. Because chances are, there is somebody out there who did the same profession first at the high caliber you could pattern your game plan after. One could research not just their career, but their (usually) humble beginnings to draw inspiration from. For many iconic people, there are innumerable books about learning from their success. For entrepreneurs, it might be advised to read "Steve Jobs" by Walter Isaacson. Or for painters, another one by the same author Leonardo da Vinci. Everyone has a calculating strategy to become better at their job than anybody, even if not in a profession where one can find untapped inspiration from. Every iconic person had to start at some time at the bottom to reach the uppermost ranks of their career. The first stepping stone would be to go to your bookseller, focus and read about them. They formulate a game plan using many of their techniques. Simple? No. Possible. Yes. If you wanna be a winner, study them.

13. Everyday Goal Oriented

Being a person with strong decision-making skills for 'the bigger picture is one step to changing your mind. By meticulous planning and organization, having self-awareness, keen time management, and detailed research and analysis of your objective, you are on a path to self-improvement. Whatever your life, astronaut, teacher, whatever, if one plans ahead and bit by bit heads towards that goal, you will be that much closer to achieving your goal. Moving closer to your lofty finish line takes using many methods but one of the keys is the aforementioned. Have a goal ahead of yourself, and in the same token of breathing, keep an optimistic mind frame. It's less about having some overnight success like winning the Powerball Jackpot; that is a Pipe-dream. It's more about heading straight and narrow towards a goal day by day. When it comes to the ups and downs of goals and how hard it is to achieve, Jerry Seinfeld said it best, "Keep your head up in failure and your head down in success."

14. Love/Be Passionate About Your Job

Finding something that that you actually enjoy helps lubricate the ball bearing to achieve your dreams. Everybody has had jobs they dislike, and those jobs are harder to find meaningful growth at. What that thesaurus type word to describe this is: passionate. It is to have a strong passion or belief for something that is the momentum for you to tackle your goals. If you're a person that dislikes writing, for instance, you can use some positive thinking and learn to enjoy sometimes Herculean endeavors of writing. Find a professional that you are passionate about, and that will be the great stepping stone to going places.

15. Being Thankful

Be thankful for what you have and take heed of what others may not. Having a sense of graciousness and a respectful person just helps cut down on some unforeseen variables: hostility. Which in effect, may give you stress and then in a chain reaction, distract you from your ultimate objectives in life. Being a Negative Nancy or a Negative Ned (or whatever they'd call the male version) of what you have and the people around you will have the opposite effect on your aching goals. Simply being thankful for what you have, and having a benign attitude to the people around you, can help build relationships and can both make you happier and also help you spearhead your goals.

16. Toughness

Achieving goals is a long row to hoe. What that takes is vigilance and determination working hand and hand. Whenever there is something that throws you a loop, I have a contingency plan that even if things go haywire, you have a way to continue to press forward to your goals. There are many hurdles one will have before one ultimately achieves, but it is a matter if you have the courage and conviction to continuously jump those hurdles, no matter how many, which is what distinguishes the winners from the losers. Bite your lower lip, and tough it out, soldiers.

17. Find a Guiding Light

Everybody has some hero. Be it Pablo Picasso, Martin Luther King, or Oprah Winfrey. The more humble the beginning of the hero is mixed with great achievements and a remarkable source of inspiration. If you have the desire to become the next great songwriter, then it's probably advised to study up on the true greats like Bob Dylan and Stevie Wonder. Or your inspiration in life can be somebody you personally know like a life coach or a parent. It is crucial to achieving goals by not just working at them, fighting throw ups and downs and zigs and zags, but also having a meaningful source of inspiration to use as a guiding light in the darkness.

18. Stay Fit, Stay Healthy

Your physical prowess correlates directly with your mental acuity. Stay in great physical condition—or at least the best you can in your situation; eating right and excessing can have direct cause and effect on your ability to grow and get that much closer to surmounting that mountain. If your body is not exactly firing on all cylinders, you are kind of in a defensive survivalist mindset, and it's harder for the main person to retain new information—much less have the motivation to head into murky waters and to learn new things. Attempt to take good care of your body, and what you put into your body, be it harmful substances, processed foods, or too much red meat, and you can have a leg up and help your mind. On a final note: the Mediterranean diet in addition to exercise, is a good one to punch to improve health.

19. Read Books

In a 2021 Pew Research survey, they found that 38% percent of Hispanic adults, 25% of Black adults, and 20% percent of white adults haven't read a book in any form in the last year. Those figures are almost triple from 1978. So if you are looking to get a leg up on your competition in the workforce, and naturally improve your mind and critical thinking skills, read books. Not just helpful guide books about neuroplasticity and brain development, but all kinds. From reading about the Ukraine War or Stephen King's book or Tony Robin's book—-all of this ties into developing your mind like a maestro conducts in the orchestra. From the MRI scan from the National Library of Medicine, that brain reading ability Brain maturation, and the circuitry become stronger and obviously more sophisticated. On the other side of the coin, people that didn't read were revealed to have less gray mattering in their brains. Various studies found a relation between the literary level and the gray and white matter in the brain. The moral of all this medical data and percentages is if you're looking to truly develop yourself, follow all of the aforementioned things but read, read, read.

20. Reduce/Eliminate Alcohol

According to the national institute of alcohol abuse and alcoholism, there are damaging effects on the brain and the more widely known cirrhosis of the liver. Drinking too much alcohol can hinder your memory after only a few drinks. Drinking too much over a long period from alcoholism can have lingering effects on the brain. It is reported that 80% of alcoholics delve into what is called Wernicke where they have a deficiency of thiamine, aka vitamin B. What this does is cause confusion and paralysis of the nerves. Over 80 or 90% of alcoholics develop Korsakoff Syndrome which is coordination, walking, and lastly, memory issues. Through brain–imaging techniques research has shown that alcoholics also hinder the growth of new brain cells. The positive twist on all of this doom and gloom: according to them, one year of abstinence shows some improvement from these lingering effects of alcoholism. Of course, there are other substances, marijuana, and all hard drugs. But research shows that all of these are doing something to the brain that will hinder your ability to grow your mind.

2.2 Summary

If you want to be the next Serena Williams, Tom Brady, or LeBron James, put in the blood, sweat, and tears and believe that you have the ability to be great. There are a lot of references to sports athletes in this chapter, and there is a reason why for them to win, they have to overcome the adversity of the swings and momentum of the game. In every single competition, game one has to have confidence, and the ability to overcome potentially losing, or coming from behind to win. And to seal the victory, you have to have a razor-like focus and ability to press on even if it looks like a losing game. If one thinks of a game a lot like a game, and sometimes you win, sometimes you lose, you keep pressing forward through positive thinking... you formulated a winners mentality.

Chapter 3: Turn a Negative Into a Positive

Neuroscientist Rick Hanson wrote in his book Buddha Brain, has a great analogy for this strange quality of the mind. "Your brain is like Velcro for negative experiences and Teflon for positive ones. Simply changing your mind from a negative frame to a positive feed can be a real difference between nailing a big job interview or just being too jittery and not confident to get one. One of the life lessons one could learn from that statement is that all phases of life turn negativity into positive energy and reign in negative thought patterns. There are many techniques that could help control the whirlwind of negative chronic worry of dark thoughts in the head. Having dark thoughts dominate your thinking will prevent you from growing to reach your maximum potential. According to psychologist Scott Bea, PsyD, there is a correlation between negative thought patterns and such mental issues as obsessive-compulsive disorder, anxiety, depression, and chronic worry. Teenagers, in particular, are stricken by habitual negative thinking. So if one is taught how to turn that ship around by reaching out about it or telling a son or daughter about it sooner, it could give them a happier youth which could blossom into a better adult. The moral of the factoid: unchained negative thoughts can make you bonkers.

The other big elephant in the room: is the little thing called negativity bias. One hundred twenty thousand years ago, this was a good thing to have when men hunted with spears were famished for food, or were chased by a rhinoceros. Negativity in the modern world, where you have the necessities at your disposal, chances are if you purchase this book, it means that a lot of negativity is not necessary for your survival. Do you want a little more motivation to squish those Negative Nancy thoughts? How about this. From the year 2004 to 2012, there was a study of seventy thousand women. John Hopkins and published in the American Journal of Epidemiology found that if you have a chipper attitude, more optimistic you have a significantly lesser risk of dying of major causes of early demise. Things such as:

- Heart disease
- Stroke
- Cancer (including ovarian, lung, breast and colorectal cancers)
- Infection
- Respiratory diseases

Some other benefits of just turning that smile upside down, and having a more positive frame form mine are also:

- better quality of life
- higher energy levels
- better psychological and physical health
- faster recovery from injury or illness
- fewer colds
- lower rates of depression
- better stress management and coping skills
- longer life span

Which transitions to the game plan to fix this dilemma of being plagued with doom and gloom thoughts. Having a simply more sunny side outlook on things will make your brain learn better but also adapt to new information better and, most obviously, make one more happy. See, in your amygdala and limbic system in the brain, we are hardwired to notice threats. In these prehistoric times of early man, our brains worked hard to have the maximum focus to not get speared by a wild bull. But in the centuries that have passed, the dangers to use are more trivial.

Losing a job. The girlfriend is angry. Maybe the Chicago Bulls lost multiple games. You can't find your phone or more serious things like a health scare. But generally speaking, the stuff they worry about makes no difference if one is stressed about it or not. Proof? According to research at Cornell University, 85% of Worries Never Happen. Of the 15% of worries that were reality, 79% of the time, people handled those situations. This translates to this hard-hitting number: 97% of our worries are pointless. In a day and age, we have 50,000 thoughts and images each day. So what can one do to help shepherd the dark ones so one can change their mind? Through measured progress, and noticing when you are ruminating in a morose web of thoughts, you can improve your psyche. These are some crucial tips to help commandeer that worst-case scenario type of thinking or in medical terms Cognitive Distortions.

3.1 Steps How Ways to Turn a Negative Into a Positive

1. Positive Mindset - There is this quote by Greek philosopher Heraclitus, "Day by day, what you choose, what you think, and what you do is who you become." Thus, Your thoughts control destiny. If you build yourself up with a positive framework. and tackle negativity with a positive psyche, you can overcome obstacles faster and slowly turn yourself into a more idealized version of yourself. It doesn't just begin with doing a lot of physical work or hours at the office or in a gym, it stems from a mindset of positive thinking. Remove negative self-talk. One of the things this also does is help reduce stress. There is a litany of things that come from just being the good sport of this thing called life. According to the Mayo Clinic, it improves a range of things in your life. First, a positive mindset increases life span and decreases depression/distress/pain. Your body's natural killer cells

have put forth a greater toughness to diseases. The no-brainer part, you will have a superior psychological and also physical body and superior cardiovascular health from disease and stroke. Lastly, reduced the risk of death from cancer, respiratory conditions, and infections. There probably is a saying you've heard dozens of times, but there is a deeper truth to it if you think about the psychological ramifications of it in the long term. So instead of thinking of that glass as half empty, think of it as half full.

2. Keep Positive People Around You - If you have people around you that are dragging you down, be it just not having a goal, substance abuse problems, or just plain 'ol Mean Girls, then you gotta find another crew. If you cocoon yourself around people that can pull you up, put their egos and insecurity aside, and they can help you become a happier person and maybe help you fulfill your goals. Avoid hanging around narrow-minded people, and find people that are open-minded. There is a saying that goes, "You are who you hang around with." That saying rings true. Here is a quote from motivational speaker Tony Robbins, "If we surround ourselves with people who are successful, who are forward-moving, who are positive, who are focused on producing results, who support us, it will challenge us to be more and do more and share more. If you can surround yourself with people who will never let you settle for less than you can be, you have the greatest gift that anyone can hope for." – Tony Robbins

3. Being Mindful of a Cauldron of Negative Thoughts - Emily K Lindsay, is a PhD researcher from the University of Pittsburgh, and John David Creswell from Carnegie Mellon University is another researcher studying mindfulness attention. The two

of them created a MAT, Monitoring and Acceptance Model. Which is to be more turned into one's thoughts and where they are leading one. Though according to their research, you are not going to actually stop negative thoughts. What it does is it helps you through meditation and remedy the situation to normalcy quicker. So when you are in a jam mentally, study up on good meditation techniques or breathing exercises to help lessen those symptoms. The first thing to learn: Mindfulness-based stress reduction.

4. Write a Journal - What this does is instead of being plagued with negative thoughts of whatnot, you have your own writing in your own words of positive things going on in your life. You can have a positive journal of things to be grateful for. But the other thing is what Abraham Lincoln called hot letters. Where he would write an angry letter cooking with a cauldron of emotions, but... not send it. What that does is release the pinup negative thoughts and forms release. So one has two options they can do. But in terms of positive thinking, the first start might be the gratitude journal.

5. Not Everything Negative Is Your Fault - This is basically when within pitch-black catacombs-like situations in life, you blame yourself. But not everything is within your control, and it's best not to jump to a Summary. Just having a positive framework of thoughts and being taught to put the blame on yourself, you will have a better collection of positive thoughts. Self-Blame during such things as a traumatic event is another thing to avoid and will only exacerbate your negative thoughts and personal development.

6. No More Catastrophizing - This is when you go on a plane west, and you think the plane will lose both engines and crash

into the Grand Canyon. It's predicting the worst-case scenario when pushed out of their cozy little comfort zone. What this does is it gives your mind and body undue stress for most likely random ho-hum activities, but it just hinders the way you can grow (or the distance you can travel). Put a lasso on those terrible thoughts, stop suffering, and put forth a positive framework that the worst possible thing that could happen is highly unlikely to happen.

7. Believe in a Positive Scenario - If you are shooting a free throw in basketball, and you already think it is not going in before you shoot... it probably is not going in. But if you, before you even shoot, tell yourself this is saying this is going in... the basketball is more likely to go in. It's because positive thinking lubricates positive outcomes. You learn to trust yourself. So if you go on a big date, and you think positively, and keep your charm, perhaps that date will be more receptive to you for the second date. What these are called: positive affirmations. When your thoughts are going off the tracks, bring them back on with positive reinforcement. One can remember in sports before the big play, a player will mutter to himself, "I got this." That is positive self-talk. Being your own personal Phil Jackson for all things life.

8. Not All Things in Life Are Black and White - Not everything is so clean cut and where one thing is perfectly good, and the other is wicked evil. If you don't get a perfect score on an algebra test doesn't mean you are not intelligent and deserve an F. Other more personal things, would be if you forget a friend's birthday, you are by default a horrible friend. That is just an extreme jump that one could just compartmentalize those thoughts as "made a mistake." Within this world, there are various shades of gray, and not all things are pitched back

and white, learn to block out the harshest extremes. Progress is about steady moves toward a lofty goal. Lots of time it takes incremental steps before you reach that Promised Land one wants.

9. Laughter Is the Best Medicine - Are your interests in life kind of on the dark side of things of horror and politics? Well, contrast that interest to tickle your funny bone. According to the National Library of Medicine, employees who had training based on humor helped reduce anxiety. There are other health benefits that studies have found, such as lowering depression and improving self-esteem and coping skills. According to the Mayo Clinic, it also stimulates organs, soothes tension, relieves pain, improves the immune system, improves mood, and helps personal satisfaction. If you are caught in the crossfire of the murky waters of life, start watching or listening to comedy to help tackle that Negative Voice in your head. One of the more interesting factoids: even if you are not in the laughing mood, you're not feeling it that day, imitating laughter can help lower your stress rate.

10. Make a Mental Note On Negative Thoughts - On July 23, 1993, in North Carolina, NBA Superstar Michael Jordan's father, James was killed in a robbery in an SUV. During his 'Above & Beyond' documentary of the 1995-1996 NBA season, Jordan talks about how his father taught him how to turn a negative into a positive. "It was a really difficult moment for me. Somehow, I kept my head high. I thought about all the things he used to tell me. Turn a negative into a positive. And here I was dealing with him in that way. It was tough." That same year he would win the MVP Award, the scoring title, the All-Star MVP, and the NBA Championship. What he did: he fought against negative thoughts and used them to fuel him. Once a

negative thought comes, don't lack it cripple your day but attempt to release it from your mind.

11. Reframe Negative Thoughts - If your negative thoughts are like a broken record, repeating and repeating and repeating, then learn to reframe them. From the Substance Abuse and Medical Health Services Administration, sponsored by the US. Department of Health & Human Services formulated this helpful guideline to augment negative thoughts with a positive twist. Building Self-Esteem: A Self-Help Guide (booklet SMA-3715) from them they devised this table of information:

Negative Thought
Positive Thought

I am not worth anything.
I am a valuable person.

I have never accomplished anything.
I have accomplished many things.

I always make mistakes.
I do many things well.

I am a jerk.
I am a great person.

I don't deserve a good life.
I deserve to be happy and healthy.

I am stupid.
I am smart.

12. Visual Images to Remove Dark Thoughts - There are many ways to get rid of that stew of negative thoughts. According to the National Library of Medicine, people with a mind that is keen on visual imagery tend to utilize it for memory performance. But not only that, using an image in your head that brings you calm, kitten, kangaroo, or that first kiss, is a good way to cleanse the mind of what nebulous thing that haunts your psyche. The other thing this can do: doesn't strengthen the imagination and the ability to retain information.

13. Zero in on What Exactly Is Giving Your Negative Thoughts - Chances are whatever you have in your mind that is negative, will make no difference in the outcome of what happens. And, chances are, it won't even happen. So localize what exactly is causing the negative thought, and look to compartmentalize it into the basements of your mind so it does not distract you. If you are feeling doomed and gloomy and have a big new job, recognize that those negative feelings will only hinder you from doing the job. Or if every time you go on a big road trip, you get nervous. But then remember each time you went on a road trip everything went fine and dandy. Whatever is bothering you, focus on it for a bit and realize it's counterproductive

14. Positive Energy Nonverbal Energy - Albert Mahrabian, an Armenian researcher, studied body language. His research found that fifty-five percent is nonverbal, thirty-eight percent is vocal, and seven percent is words. This means communicating positive energy and looking to surround yourself with people with equal positive energy for your own self-confidence. Simply communicating more positively, even with your body language, your gait, and your posture can help

take care of your glum spirit. Neurotransmitters like serotonin, endorphins, and dopamine, all positive meddles in the brain, can be activated by doing one simple thing: smile. See, when you smile, your mind releases molecules that are named neuropeptides. What these do: they can help ward off anxiety. It creates a ripple effect by both making you feel better and also helping you connect to people from that non-verbal signal. The moral of this story is if you got a frown, well…. try turning it upside down.

15. Blue - If your mind pitches black, then remember this: B.L.U.E. If after this you're still spiraling into negative thoughts there is one last tip. Ever wanted something simple, perhaps for a child or teenager, to remember to avoid self blame? Well, this is a psychology acronym standing for things to be mindful of.

B- Blaming myself;

L - Looking for the bad news;

U - Unhappy guessing;

E - Exaggeratedly negative.

3.2 Summary

These are some no-brainer trips to help improve a person's thought process. They can improve the positivity in your mind, accomplishments, and Self-Esteem. If you are a person caught in a real pitch-black place in life, and thinking of hurting yourself, or others, contact a counselor immediately, and you can turn your life around. In summary of this segment of this book, the key to turning off negative thoughts is catching them and then turning that into a positive one.

Chapter 4: Growth Mindsets Vs. Fixed Mindsets

Professor Carol Dweck was the psychologist who invented the term "Growth Mindset." Her study is about human motivation. She also won the APA Award for Distinguished Scientific Contributions to Psychology and thus knows a thing or two about just expanding your horizons in your psyche. What she did is found the distinguishing characteristics between a person with a growth mindset and those gridlocked in a fixed mindset. Psychologist Dr. Carol Dweck did various studies on high school students to pick their brains and understand the aforementioned mindsets. In a study just after Star Wars came out in 1978, she did two studies on 130 5th-grade children using a variety of difficulty-level puzzles. Some of the students embraced the difficulty and failure and thought of the harder puzzles as learning. They were optimistic. It's at this point that she put the phrase 'Growth mindset' on the psychology map.

This study ways in which a person with an open mind takes in information, cogitates in their cranium, and uses it for their self-improvement. Then there is the devil's advocate, the person that rejects it and believes people are just born with the ability and just stay stagnant and don't develop or... at a glacier's pace. It's really the question of nature versus nurture. These characteristics are established at a very young age and are both conscious and subconscious. But the truth of the matter is, growing is a lot of nurture. Simply being in a growth-mind frame it is believed you can increase your intelligence and talents using intense perseverance. But if you are in a fixed mindset, according to Dr. Dweck, those aspects cannot be developed. It's like four feet stuck in cement, and you can't move. Silence used to say the brain stops growing in adulthood, but in reality, the muscle in our skull never stops growing neurons. It's always changing its plasticity. But in terms of a growth mindset, to actually improve and grow skills one must have the tenacity to get the boldness of temerity. So here is a rudimentary breakdown of the difference between the two mindsets.

Growth Mindset - The name applies exactly what it is, but there is more to it than that. They know it will be a long row to hoe but they know perseverance is the key. It is a steadfast belief that your intelligence and skills improve with handwork. It's a willingness to take a calculating risk for self-improvement, where failure is possible. It's a belief that blood, sweat, and tears of handwork will lead to mastering skill. People within this frame of mind also look for role models to pattern their course of action after. The big thing: they see feedback as a way to improve and is crucial for their goals. They subscribe to the idea of lifelong learning. A growth mindset remains underfed to rejection but just keeps pressing on with optimism.

Fixed Mindset - These are people that see that talented people are just innately 'born' with ability. Their personalities see failure as catastrophic, they are shamed, they wallow in despair, and they give up easily if they don't have the whole deck in their favor. They like to sidestep challenges to avoid them. They see the success of other people and get a spark of jealousy and see them as threatening. The little feedback is like a personal vendetta against them. Their personalities give up easily with a pessimistic attitude.

Psychologist Dr. Carol Dweck also found some interesting other juicy nuggets of information: obviously, growth-minded kids had increased performance—-that's a no-brainer. Their minds are open; they know failure is a learning process and can re-strategize. She found that, in particular, kids in science and mathematics would especially have a marked improvement in grades. But they also found something else: people in a growth thinking pattern had reduced burnout, less depression, anxiety and psychological problems, and behavior problems. Meaning, for your livelihood, having a growth mindset for things called life is for your good. The University of Groningen created this helpful chart of what to watch for to get out of the shackles of Fix Mindset.

Situation
Fixed mindset approach
Growth mindset approach
You get a very high grade on an exam
Great! I must be really intelligent in this area
Great! I must have worked hard and learned a lot
You're starting a new assignment or project
I hope this will be easy for me
I hope this will be interesting!
You get negative feedback on your work
Oh no! This proves I'm no good at this
Okay, I need to get back to work and learn more

As the writer of the book, one has to naturally subscribe to the notion of a growth mindset. This profession requires a constant learning process, new words, new topics, new images, and a healthy dose of failure. That is the nature of what it is to be a writer. But that mindset is a good mindset to have for all professions.

There is the part of the book where you will expand your neuroplasticity and learn a bit about significant mumbo jumbo—bear with me, nonmedical people. The National Library of Medicine found Using Hypnotherapy and neuroimaging. These scientists measured that people with growth mindset brains are more active and have more focus on the process of doing it... rather than the end adult. They also found they are more apt to change course. All are key attitudes to development.

4.1 Steps How To Get Into a Growth Mindset:

A person can change their hard work and grit. Neuroscience reveals that your brain is malleable. It changes its plasticity through experiences and info. It also strengthens connections but in the same instant, grows new ones. It also reveals neurons are constantly growing in the brain. This means in layman's terms: you can change. So the million-dollar question is, how does one become a growth-minded person? Here are some basic principles to foster growth.

1. Determine What Your Mindset

Judging by the fact you purchased a book on growing your mind, chances are you are in a growth mindset. But if not, look inward, into your thoughts and maybe the pessimism you may have, and determine what you are, Fixed or Growth. As for your questions, how you could make calculating struggles to improve yourself. One of the other great benefits of being within a growth mindset is the ability to enter new fields through sheer will power and open-mindedness.

2. Understand 'Not Yet'

You are not a _____... yet. Think of the power in that three-letter word. How you could maybe get incredible failure from all angles, but if you simply tell yourself that you have a fighting chance for the next time around. It also rewires your mental pattern to see more of a long game at hand, not a short-term victory. The aforementioned pioneering psychologist in this mental framework, Dr. Dweck mentioned in her TED conference just how powerful the word Yet is. So if you have a series of hurdles, down on your luck, say to yourself not yet when you are looking to get your goals. It brings a degree of optimism that your goal is still within your grasp.

3. Take Pleasure in the Process

Whatever you're trying to do, if you learn to somehow converse with yourself to enjoy it then you have a better shot at improving at it. Simply learn to appreciate the handwork it takes, maybe the setbacks, and see the Growth Mindset journey as one Nintendo big game too, and things don't always work out your way. There is a saying, "it is not about the destination… it's about the journey.

4. Silence the Fix Mindset Voice

If you have the voice of George Costanza from Seinfeld in your head, that pessimistic attitude, learn to silence him. That negative Cognitive Distortions voice hinders your ability to have a growth mindset. This thinking pattern consumes a person with negativity and pessimism. Simply put: they are Hijacking Your Brain. There are a range of ways to fix this voice; hypnosis is one of them. Or just be mindful of that inner George Costanza in your head at all times. Say to yourself, "You can do this." Instead of "I can't do this." Even if it comes up short, it's a learning process, and you can try, try, and try again.

5. All Research Says You Can

As noted throughout this book, medical scientists used to think the brain could not grow, but then they learned quite the contrary. That is Scientific data proving that you can indeed develop your brain through neuroplasticity. The first chapter covers many techniques of ways to reinforce brain plasticity that same info works in spades for this area. Learn to get out of your comfort zone, that same beaten path. Challenge yourself to take control of your brain one day at a time.

6. Constructive Feedback

Whenever you produce something, be it a new sales technique, writing, Photoshop work, or an invented new Version of Astroturf, get some feedback on that. Listen to your peers, your parents, your customers, your clients, or whoever is there near you. Sometimes, people that are a bit too close to you may be skittish to offer the bluntest feedback you need. So seek a perfect stranger to what they think, and then do not get defensive… listen. Then re-strategize, if needed.

7. Get Out of Your Comfort Zone

This is a constantly repeated slogan on how to Change Your Mind. It's all about spearheading northward into untreated growth. If you don't like reading about medical science, it's hard to learn (for instance), well, learn about it, and maybe it can be informative. Not just with information but with how you move about the world. Instead of bike riding in loops around the park, venture onward into the city. It's a small thing like that, and repeating them, is how you grow and change your psyche for the betterment of your own good.

8. Make Mistakes

Part of getting out of your comfort zone is accepting mistakes will happen. But if you are in a growth-minded position, then you know that those mistakes are wondrous opportunities to learn and re-strategize. Nobody is perfect, and there have been a lot of mistakes and failures throughout history, but one thing is consistent failure can make you better if you learn to adjust course and learn. Be persistent and cultivate a Challenge.

9. Failure Is Part of the Growth Process

Academical ability isn't the only measuring stick of where you will go in life; it's also about handling failure correctly and steadfast perseverance. This is a memorable quote from legendary basketball player Micheal Jordan. "I've missed more than 9,000 shots in my career. I've lost almost 300 games. Twenty-six times I've been trusted to take the game-winning shot and miss. I've failed over and over and over again in my life. And that is why I succeed." It's the act of trying again and again, and perhaps failing again, that distinguishes the winners from the losers. See failure as deliberate practice for eventual success. You can be an F student and get the A life with just how you handle failure and what you do with it.

10. Be a Fan of Yourself

As narcissistic as it sounds, you gotta be your own buddy if you're gonna be venturing out into uncharted waters where rejection is possible. Having feelings of self-loathing is just going to exacerbate the obvious ups and downs that happen in life. Everybody has deficiencies and what is important is to be mindful of your positives. The world can be tough for you but do not also be tough on yourself too, which will only bring a negative voice in your head. Think of your positive attributes or your previous achievements to mitigate the melancholy feeling of failure. Be a fan of your work, if raw, see the positive part of it and also see the positive part of your own self. To have a growth mindset, try to develop a more optimistic disposition through all of life's obstacles.

11. Do Goldilock Tasks

These are things you could do that are not extremely difficult, and they are not easy peasy either. They are just outside of your familiar comfort zone, and they offer a challenge. That way, if you do it, you will not give up it will be a challenge but not exhausting. Find something that you can do that can expand your skill set for continuous improvement. Doing enough of these and never giving up can help shift your mindset to something that will promote meaningful growth.

12. Have Goals

If you are in a growth mindset, try to have some type of end game rather than just learning and expanding your horizons. The reason? It can be a strong motivation technique to spearhead you forward. Maybe, acquiring a certain score on some time of the test. Or, sales goal. Or maybe selling your first novel. Or, more realistically, getting a positive review from somebody. Then if you brainstorm a realistic, tangible goal, and visualize achieving that goal in your head, it helps it become more realized and possible. Just make sure and remember to set realistic goals and not to be a billionaire at 25 or give up on said Growth Mindset.

In closing, that is all the various steps for this segment. Being in the right frame of mind would also help develop entrepreneur skills where the completion is already re-strategizing and helps with resilience and keeping one grounded. Because in this thing called life, the pendulum swings different ways. A group of Fortune 1000 companies such as Apple, GE, Bloomberg, Microsoft, Uber, and Pinterest have all used their mindset for positive business growth. Here is some data from the study on why fostering growth is paramount for companies in the tech sector. This is what their data found:

- 47% more invested in their work
- 34% higher commitment to the company
- 47% more trust in the company
- 49% stronger belief that their company encourages innovation, which is essential to growth

These conglomerate companies like Apple and Microsoft have created a culture for limitless growth. Where calculated risks are good, and learning from failure is essential. Having a growth-minded approach to life gives you mental agility for innovation and is absolutely crucial for any budding entrepreneur. Professional Dweck remarked that focusing on people that are motivated by a challenge, working with people, and wanting to grow is more important than pedigree. If your company is within this thought pattern, it might be a good time for culture-shaping ignorer to gain a competitive advantage in the marketplace. Perhaps the greatest blunder by any company that uses the Fix mindset Vs. Growth mindset: It was Jan. 9, 2007, when Steve Jobs announced the first generation iPhone. It was a landmark device that changed, well, the whole world (for good or bad). It had a capacitive touch screen, a desktop-like web browser, an iPod, and a camera. It was the biggest break in tech since the personal computer. Even naysayers will have to admit that the iPhone changed the industry in one fell swoop.

But one thing to make a note of: the mindset differences between Microsoft's reaction and Google's reaction tectonic shift in the technology marketplace. At the time, they were knee-deep and working on their Android platform as something more similar to a BlackBerry with a keyboard they were looking to release soon. They had prototypes that were similar to Blackberry. But midway through Steve Jobs's meticulously planned presentation, they saw that was clearly the Next Generation of phones and the future.

Google saw the presentation and was floored. They scrapped their Blackberry knockoffs and went directly into making a phone like an iPhone. That was an example of a growth mindset. On the flip side, is Microsoft. They were at the time, the leader in the up-and-coming smartphone business. Microsoft CEO Steve Ballmer was dismissive of the iPhone. "Five hundred dollars? Fully subsidized? With a plan? I said that is the most expensive phone in the world." Then he said, "And it doesn't appeal to business customers because it doesn't have a keyboard. Which makes it not a very good email machine." Steve Ballmer said. Microsoft had the marketplace in an iron grip, and he was clearly in a fixed mindset. They were not looking to advance the phone to the next level but be complacent with their instantly dated Windows Mobile software... that blunder caused Microsoft to release their capacitive touch screen Windows phone years too late to the game. Meanwhile, because Google was in a growth mindset, they saw what the future held; they released Android within a year or iPhone's launch. Right now, Android and iPhone are neck and neck in market share in the US, with iPhone having a bit of advancement. Because Microsoft released too late and was in a fixed mindset, its platform never gained traction because it didn't have enough developer support. As Bill Gates said with software, "It's winner takes all."

This is why in business, it is crucial to be in a growth mindset and recognize the competition and not be dismissive of it.

4.2 Summary

As if you are a common person, not a multimillionaire tech guru, and just looking to get a leg up in life, these pillars for improvement to a growth mindset help you blossom. As with many things, if your chips are down, one has to go into a growth phase to get back on track. To fully comprehend all of the complexes of this, look into Carol Dweck's 2006 book, Mindset: The New Psychology of Success. Where she covered in intricate detail how she stumbled upon this discovery and gave additional information on how and can improve their mindsets on whether their chips are down or up in life. All of these elements are a cornerstone of self-improvement.

Chapter 5: How To Connect The Brain and Soul to Gain Mastery Over Emotional Intelligence

Aristotle wrote, "Some men . . . if they have first perceived and seen what is coming and have first roused themselves and their calculative faculty, are not defeated by their emotion, whether it be pleasant or painful." The key part to take out of that: is the defeat by their emotional part.

For centuries as far back as 350 B.C.E, Psychologists and philosophers thought cognition and emotion were separate. With the stand-fast idea that emotion hinders productivity. Like Mr. Spock in Star Trek, it is emotion versus sound logic. If you have emotion, you compromise yourself and your ability to think. But over time, psychologists learned they are in the same domain of understanding; they are interrelated and are essential for forming empathy and understanding oneself.

So what is EQ? In one sentence; it's the perception of your and others' emotions and then the ability to facilitate critical thinking. In three words: it's the management of emotions. Professional Thorndike in the Jazz era of the 1920s, coined the term social intelligence. It described it as, the "ability to understand and manage men and women, boys and girls, to act wisely in human relations." This history of the exact phase of Emotional Intelligence was pioneered in 1990, by John D. Mayer of UNH and Peter Salovey of Yale, two psychology professors. What their research paper covered was introducing the world to what is EQ. In simple terms, It is the ability to understand your emotions and others more efficiently. It is that cognition and emotion are connected, and one can discriminate a course of action from them. It is the ability to intricately understand people's emotional welfare used to mitigate stress, understand others and communicate, empathize with others, overcome difficult tasks and lessen conflict. Having a pinpoint understanding of emotions simply makes you a more efficient person.

An adequate understanding of EQ can help you with a range of things in life. Notwithstanding, successes in work and school, career, and building stronger connections with people by being more empathetic to their feelings. If you have the ability to understand not just your own emotions and intelligently change course, you can do the same with your interaction with people to be more efficient and shrewd decision-makers. The four pillars of EQ are the following:

Self-Management - It's to control your emotions, and saviors and manage your and others' feelings in positive ways. Using critical thinking skills to take initial emotional understanding, and the ability to adjust from understanding. It's to thoughtfully read emotions. This is also called self-perceived emotional intelligence (PEI).

Self-Awareness - It's to understand one's feelings and see how others detect those feelings you express. Understanding your own Achilles heel, your weakness, and having self-assurance upon understanding them.

Social Awareness - In social situations, it's to be a social butterfly and feel comfortable. You are empathetic and have concerns for people, and can pick up on social cues. You can see the power structure of groups and adjust accordingly.

Relationship Management - A team player who works well within a group and can mitigate conflict. Because of interpersonal skills, and empathy, you foster solid relationships. To each person, you are a good speaker, and because of that, you can inspire others.

Why Is EQ So Important?

Early man's common ancestor, Neanderthals, had to worry about hunting, finding shelter, and language skills were primitive at best. But thousands of years later, a crucial component is communication and understanding people. According to the National Library of Medicine, older adolescents, non-homeless people, and homeless older adolescents have similar IQs except for their verbal skills are slightly lesser. You can be an exemplary student but have poor social skills, and that could be your downfall by not understanding how vital EQ is. If that doesn't confine you, here are some other bullet points to inspire you. The other big thing to take out of this: according to research from the National Library of Medicine, EQ plays into happiness and lower EQ plays into being bullied in school.

Career/ Academic Performance

Your performance is interwoven with your understanding of people's emotions and how you can change accordingly. Prime example: interviews. EQ comes into play in that face-to-face meeting and many others where you are put under scrutiny by a stranger. If you have a firm grasp of sensibility to feelings, you can interact with people better and build bonds. Whenever you are hired for many jobs they have you do a computer test. What they are testing: your personality and emotional intelligence and how you interact with others. In the leadership position, a high Emotional intelligence correlates with organizational effectiveness.

Physical Health - Being plagued with stress and anxiety takes a toll on the heart and blood pressure, and immune system. Self-regulating emotions can help reading yourself and also learn how to de-escalate stressful situations. In addition, according to the National Library of Medicine, the lower the EQ, the higher the chances of phobias and self-harm. Critical thinking about your emotions and changing thought patterns can help you live longer. So whether you are in a high-stress personal situation, or dealing with an ill-tempered person, you could use EQ and look to decompress from the stress and preserve your own body....

Mental Health - Your mind and body work hand-in-hand. If you are a person that continuously spearheads into high-stress situations, when you can avoid them can get better results, that is where EQ could help. Having the skill set to reign in your worst impulses and thoughtfully communicate with people can help you from suffering from mental illnesses such as depression. Simply not interacting well with people can give you depression, and then you can spiral downward even more.

Relationship - People can come across as complex, no matter what their gender is. Having a firm understanding of understanding people's emotions, by it by their body language, minor social cues, fluctuations in voice or what they actually say, and anything in-between can help you foster relationships. Most of all, it helps you with your networking skills which are crucial for people in particular white-collar jobs, but it's also essential for anybody looking to methodically build connections. EQ plays highly in developing long-term relationships.

Social Intelligence - Having a precise understanding of your emotions and others helps in social situations. Company meetings, school interaction, team chemistry, all of it. Developing an understanding of social intelligence will help you understand who is one you can connect to, and not. Having a degree of intelligence of people's emotions in social gatherings can help you interact, lower stress and find love and prolong connections.

How To Develop Your EQ?

As Mahatma Gandhi once said, "Speak only if it improves upon the silence." If you want to develop your emotional intelligence, one has to begin to use critical thinking skills to understand your own emotions and others and then learn to change. Learn to defuse conflict situations and take out your stress on yourself. Understand your psyche and how emotion and judgment go hand and hand in each social interaction you have. Seek to build your social skills, perhaps listen more if you are a person who talks a lot, and learn to become empathetic with each encounter you have with a person. Listen to the rhythms of conversations, the body language, the tone of voice, the topics, and how you can interact with people more succinctly. Learn to be simpatico with other people.

Here are some things to look for to develop your EQ;

Self-regulation

Scenario: In a game of pick-up basketball, a player calls a foul that seems not to be a foul at all.
Higher EQ: You listen and agree with the foul in a way to see the bigger picture that it is just a pickup game of basketball. The relationship with the team is important.
Lower EQ: You get enraged and throw the basketball at the player and create an award situation for everybody on the court.

Empathy

Scenario; A girlfriend is not happy you forget her birthday and didn't even get her a card.

Higher EQ; You explain a legitimate why and apologize. You make up for it by doing something special for her.

Lower EQ: You brush it off, and do not understand why a woman must get a card on their birthday and don't understand their sensitivity for gift cards.

Self-Awareness

Scenario: You are at an off-hours company meeting, and there is a dress code.

Higher EQ: You wear exactly what you are supposed to wear and look to interact with others. You rarely do not use your phone.

Lower EQ: You wear something you are not supposed to, remain rebellious from the group, and play with your phone in a self-absorbed manner.

Motivation:

Scenario: You're looking to publish a book about Changing Your Mind.

High EQ: You tough through it, write a helpful book, and am grateful for anything that happens.

Lower EQ: You give up realizing writing a book is difficult and may not be a New York Times Best Seller.

Social Skills:

Scenario: You have a job interview tomorrow to be a software engineer at Apple.

High EQ: You make eye contact, firm handshake, answer questions well, and smile often.

Lower EQ: You do not make contact, have a weak handshake and answer questions non-efficiently and have a dour expression.

5.1 Steps How To Build Emotional Intelligence

1. Be Outgoing and Assertive

If you are a wallflower personality, try to be assertive and get out of your shell. Extend ourselves to make tangible connections to people. Instead of being the person standing in the corner, go into the group and talk. Start small, and work your way up. Practice understanding non-verbal cues and modulating your voice to show expression. Look to come out of your shell and harmonize with a group. Cultivate, creating more connections.

2. Handle Conflict With Ease

People with High-EQ know how to handle conflict. Sometimes it is just about keeping your voice mellow and your body language composed. Learn to handle each stressful encounter like a riddle you must solve the answer to. Understand sometimes you want a resolution, but other times it is best just to walk away knowing it's impossible to compromise with the person. Pick your battles wisely, and chances are unless it's a matter of life and death, no battle might be the best alternative.

3. Be A Expert Listener

"Change happens by listening and then starting a dialogue with the people who are doing something you don't believe is right." – Jane Goodall. Many people with Low-EQ only half-listen to what the other person says, wait for the person to stop talking, then talk. If one slows things down, and for a real rapport with the other and what they are saying, you can create a bond with them. Many people simply are not given full attention. Not only that, the person should take a greater liking to you if you listen with your ears open.

4. Be Motivated

People that have emotional intelligence firing on all cylinders, put forth a goal you could have to energize you throughout the day. Seek various goals you could have, not just one. Sometimes growth comes from increments, ups, and downs, but one must look at the bigger picture to see progress. Use emotional intelligence to understand your emotions when things are not working your way.

5. Practice Having a Positive Frame of Mind

If you have a positive attitude when interacting with people, be it smile, topic, or body language it can be infectious to draw people towards you. Merely having a positive outlook helps you harness connections and develop even more positive growth. Having an understanding that your body language is more than half of your communication with people... and a lot of people can see if you are on the positive or negative spectrum by your body language. Keep a sunny-side optimistic spirit at all times. The glass IS half full, remember.

6. Self Awareness

. Emotionally intelligent people know of the vibe they are giving off and can change it. If you are having a bad day, be self-aware to try not to project that, be cheerful, or you will push people away from you. Everybody has a bad day, but how you handle it is the difference between Low-EQ and High-EQ. If you realize you are going 'out of the pocket,' go right back in to help foster connections and mitigate alienation. Have an awareness of one's faults and seek to correct them using practices.

7. Handle Feedback With Grace

Everybody (probably) has gotten a score they wish they have never gotten. It hurt. Maybe it drags your day down into the dumpster. But how you handle it says a lot about your personality. Lebron James lost in the NBA Finals twice before we won an NBA Championship. He also had a series of setbacks in other series. What he did is he got better and listened to the criticism from the media that he wasn't assertive enough and needed to develop a low-post game. Through measured strides, and listening, he got better So even the greats are criticized. Success in life comes from how you tackle failure.

8. Look To Understand People's Feelings.

Each person has a different story, and many people are full of hardships, and maybe people never know. If you see a person angry for trivial things, there is probably a reason why in their personal life. Look to see people as books that one could empathize with, even if they are very different from you. Look to read people's feelings using EQ and share common ground to help create bonds. If you find a self-absorbed person, try to find out why. Or Vice versa.

9. Develop Leadership Skills

Leaders have a certain panache about them. They take charge. They are insertive. They listen. They have humor. Their personalities are bold. That is the skillset one should look to develop to fully utilize emotional intelligence training. If you are a reserved person who it's too absorbed in the computer, realize it's gonna take probably years to develop that skill. But the path begins with one first step.

10. Understand The Power of First Impressions

How you are dressed, how you communicate, and your facial features are all some of the first impressions that people get from you. Learn to be approachable and learn how to disarm people if you may come across as intimidating. Have an understanding that nonverbal communication is over half of communication and many people are kind of shy, especially in certain fields. Learn to have people drawn to you by a sense of humor and cheek to cheek smile.

5.2 Summary

All of these are many skills that can help you build the foundations of changing your mind and also developing a high emotional intelligence. As noted, you're not exactly gonna be a social butterfly and have a mastery of emotional intelligence overnight. To be blunt, it may take years for you to fully come out of your shell if you're a person who struggles with self-confidence. But with determination, understanding of human psychology, continuous motivation, and utilizing the teachings of emotional intelligence... you could be well on your way.

Chapter 6: Natural Brain Detoxes and How Sleep Is a Key Component of Learning

There is lifespan, and then there is brainpan. Which means, how long your brain can stay in peak homeostasis performance. The following information on how vital sleep is to peak mental health—-and perhaps the most important chapter in the whole book on brain health. This is the part of the book where the author will dry to avoid quick remedies and wonder drugs. The primary reason is your liver and kidney, and a little thing called sleep care or detoxification. Within your brain is the glymphatic system, and the rest of the body's system is called the lymphatic, minus the G. Glymphatic was only named in 2013 as the central nervous system (CNS) of vertebrates, a way of removing waste. The term glymphatic system was invented by Maiken Nedergaard, a Danish neuroscientist. Without getting overly medical here with too much neuroscience mumbo-jumbo, this helps reduce soluble proteins and metabolites and waste to your body on these things called (big word) perivascular channels. The brain must be within a form of the cavity (sleep works too) to remove potentially neurotoxic waste from the mind for homeostasis (healthy brain). It helps the brain cleanse parenchymal tissue (covering). Chances are, this info is a lot to take in, but it's not as difficult as it sounds. The brain is a muscle with fluids and blood flow and needs to be restored. Which transitions to the topic of the chapter: detoxification. Other things, what you look for your when the brain needs detox Some of the issues when your brain is overworked is problems with brain fog (A "Long Covid" symptom), fatigue, and memory loss, (All common issue with people who had Covid-19) depression, head injury, stroke, addiction, and nerve-wracking anxiety. If your brain has all of these caveats going on, it's time to detox, pronto First, except for stroke, this is the logical solution to no-pills, no-frills restorative treatment of your brain. What more motivation? Having an understanding of this and taking action can reduce the likelihood of neurodegenerative diseases like Alzheimer's. One other thing, when we sleep, we increase glymphatic activity to remove more waste from our brain. The first thing on the oodles of steps to help promote detoxification of your is a little thing called meaningful restorative sleep.

6.1 Ways to Detox The Brain

1. Sleep

There have been endless studies on just how crucial sleep is to the brain. One of the biggest things it does is not just feeling refreshed to tackle your day, but to your overall physical and mental prowess and most of all, removing toxic molecules and also the removal of unwanted proteins. This is according to Dr. Phyllis Zee, a professor of neurology at Northwestern University Feinberg School of Medicine. The average person sleeps 6.5 hours per night, yet the National Sleep Foundation says healthy adults need 7-9 hours per night. That gap between the two affects the ability to learn. Dr. Matthew Walker, Neuroscientist and Psychology at the University, and also the Founder and Director of the Center for Human Sleep of California, goes into detail about how crucial sleep is to your brain and overall health. For the hippocampus to properly encode learning and memories, you need seven to nine hours of sleep. It has been researched less than optimal sleep decreases learning by 40 percent. Sleep is, quite simply, a 'Save Button' for memory. What various studies have learned is REM sleep helps you embed information that you learned into your brain. Deep Sleep, according to Dr. Walker, is about gathering your knowledge together. But REM sleep is about processing it subconsciously to engrain memory into the neural architecture of the brain. Just to belabor the point, There is a saying, "Sleep on it." But that saying has scientific data saying that is, in fact, true. If you have a problem, you can have dream-inspired insight into how to solve the problem. Dmitri Mendeleev, an early 18th-century Russian chemist, invented the periodic table of elements, a way to display chemical elements (Li, Cs, Ac, etc.) from dream inspiration. Auto Loi won the Nobel Peace Prize through chemical transpiration through nerve cells from dream inspiration. Probably the most widely known story of dream inspiration is when Paul McCartney dreamed of the melody to the song Yesterday. Each of those examples was men who used sleep for problem-solving and little creativity. However, it is more likely, your brain will be more mentally engrossed in solving the problem in the morning, not by any epiphany like a dream like a Beatle but more just from getting proper rest—it is crucial to brain health and retaining information. Just like clicking Command + S on your keyboard to save a Word document—-that's why slumber does. How to respect to retain the information you learn, much less from this book, if your brain is too exhausted to retain it?

Example: Integration of relational memory testing. According to a study posted on Springer (a leading global scientific publisher on topics of Cognitive, Affective, & Behavioral Neuroscience) in 2011, they reported that sleep helps you retain your memory but also catalogs "relational memories." During an experiment, people were tested on the impact of insomnia on the cognitive thinking of the brain. (Ellenbogen et al., 2007, as cited in Walker, 2009). During this, people were taught 5 paired associates, relational pairs, and direct associates of letters. They are called premise pairs of the following A>B, B>C, C>D, and D>E. The group was not told of the overreaching hierarchy, and they were put into 3 groups. The group that slept in-between had 25% retaining the information. Sleep is key in decision-making.

Furthermore, there are lingering effects of not getting enough sleep, such as the massive drop in Natural Kills Cells and your overall body's immune system and warding off mental illnesses like Alzheimer's, cancers, preventing diabetes, regulation of blood sugar, joints, and a healthy heart. In the most simple terms of the common tongue, Everything is tied to sleep and managing a healthy circadian rhythm and healthy sleep routine. So, if you want to boost your brain and retain the information you learned today and within this book? Sleep 7-9 hours a night.

2. Quality Anti-Inflammatory Foods

There is a saying, "we are what we eat." Another one is, " We are what we consume." You get the point. What you put into your body, be it the overzealous amount of processed food or a healthy Mediterranean diet of fish, vegetables, and fruits, each plays a critical rule in your cognitive performance and synapse and connections in your brain. Also, just like the above topic, it ties into how well your organs work and also helps with focus, lowering depression and anxiety and boosting free radicals and antioxidants for peak body function. These are some recommendations to consume to not just help your physiological and psychological functions:

- The Mediterranean diet
- Fruits
- Vegetables
- Fish
- Shellfish
- Seaweed
- Seeds
- Yogurts
- Herbs
- Spices

- Tarmac
- Talic
- Rosemary
- Yogurts and other probiotic foods
- Nuts and seeds
- Honey
- Legumes and beans
- Chocolate
- Tea
- Coffee

In terms of that last one, Coffee is a psychoactive stimulant. According to the National Library of Medicine, coffee increases the body's energy metabolism within the brain and reduces blood flow from hypoperfusion and something called noradrenaline for the fight-or-flight response. It energizes you and also makes you happier through a hormonal chemical called dopamine. So coffee makes you feel good and also makes your brain sharper—-but use it in moderation. The sleep segment goes into the dangers of insomnia. But one thing people do not realize: according to sleep research, 25% of the caffeine in coffee is still in your body 12 hours later. This means coffee will get you sharper, but it says in the body for so long it will affect the quality of your sleep. So be mindful when using it and make sure you are fully rested in the morning, revitalized, or cut back on consumption of this psychoactive stimulant. How powerful coffee is in terms of varies by individual sensitivity? In terms of going into more detail, there are tons of books to learn about eating a proper diet. The best is to try to stick to more of the Mediterranean diet, more fish, more nuts, more vegetables and fruit. Look for food with anti-inflammatory, antioxidant, and anti-carcinogenic effects to help assist your brain. Finally, try to eat simple sustenance from products of Mother Earth and not from a factory. (Drugs and heavy alcoholic drinks are still and) For example, stuff without five or six-syllable words in the nutritional facts. So these are just some basics, and one can assume all adults know what quality food is and what is processed junk. But what you put into your body helps your brain and promotes vascular health.

3. Be Aware of Technology Addiction

Your way of being aware of your surroundings comes from early man and his desire to be aware of his surroundings in the grass savannah or the jungle. It is called the fight-or-flight response. Their body releases this hormone called cortisol to keep them hyper-aware, so they are eaten by a marauding pack of lions and scavenge for food off the bone and shelter. Flash forward 2 million years to the rise of the addictive properties of the Smartphone. Whenever you put your phone down, the adrenal gland in the brain releases that same cortisol that is tied to that flight or flight response. It is documented that we check out the phone every 15 minutes throughout the day. When you don't check your phone, your brain develops cortisol, and it starts to make you anxious like a lurking predator is on the attack or your body needs food. Rather than using that flight or flight response to attack, hunt and run, it's being used to keep you addicted by way of understanding the brain like a neurogenesis scientist.

Silicon Valley is basically brain-hacking people to become addicted to social media. They use algorithms and are finally adept at reading every keyword that you approve of to sell your advertisement but in addition, curating your content gets you consistently more addicted. On phones nowadays, there are activity monitors to restrict how much you are using them, which could benefit your brain from being distracted with addictive nonsense all day. There is a 60 Minutes episode from April 2017 with a Google developer where he gives insight into a system that is hijacking people's attention. He compares it to having a slot machine in your hand, a "Race to the bottom of the brainstem." and you keep using it no matter how unhealthy it is to your psyche. So if you see yourself constantly scrolling Instagram, Twitter, or Facebook, half a self-awareness to that cortisol release, shut it off and do something more rejuvenating to your brain.

4. Appreciate the Greater Outdoors

This is a great way to remove the toxicity of a frazzled web of emotions out of your brain... casual nature walks. Almost forty people were put in a scientific study to determine the health benefits of nature and external factors For 50 minutes. According to the National Library of Medicine, walking improves your condition, relieves stress, and also increases gratitude to detox your mind.

Simply taking a 10 to 20-minute walking brain through a forest, near a lake, or beach can help you foster new ideas and creativity but also simply clean your mind of whatever stress you may have lurking in the background. It is also noted that employers that have met in great outdoors have employees more engaged with positive rapport with one another, and it cuts down on the internal brick-and-mortar distractions of copy machines, cooks, or whatever misc sounds that may come into play in an indoor meeting. There are various reasons why you should be taking a brief time outside to detox your brain. On an additional note, if you own a dog...you are forced to go on scenic walks, and that may be something to consider.

5. Expand Real Life Social Network

In the age of Internet social networks, everybody's building friendships through that method, especially the younger crowd.

But building real connections to people or you could see personally doing activities is a good way to relieve the toxicity out of your brain and naturally relieve stress and is intrinsic to happiness. If you are miserable and things are going well, this is the logical first step to bring your emotions into more of a positive mindset in your friendship with people. If you are down in the dumps, depressing and full of whirlwind toxic thoughts and little connection to a not spoken friend in a while can help detoxify your brain. A University of Chicago researcher did a study on people talking to strangers on buses, strangers or being mute. Well, talking to strangers is... better than talking to nobody and will help bring a crucial dopamine release. So if you are a lone wolf, or maybe a social butterfly, expanding your network of friends—positive friends, can help detoxify your brain and bring about homeostasis (good mine) and work that glymphatic system in your mind for brain health.

6. Reduce Toxin Exposure

Like a lurking leviathan in the deep, there are chemicals all over lurking beyond just household products. It's Everywhere. Make a calculating effort to consume more organic products. Avoid plastics, pesticides (wash food), carcinogen-laced weed killers, beauty products, and cleaning products. Stop using plastic bottles and look for "BPA-Free" labeling. Wash hands often. Make a calculating attempt to mitigate the consumption of toxicity in your life. Use a vacuum with a HEPA filter. The water filter company Brita, has made excellent filters to either put on your tap directly or pour pitcher to help remove toxicity in the water. Another tip, in order to mitigate pesticides from the grass on the bottom of your shoe, take them off when you come into your house. These are various techniques to curtail your body from consuming unnecessary toxic exposure throughout the world.

7. Exercise But Also Stay Hydrated

Last but not least, is the no-brainer to detoxing. This topic is covered above so one doesn't need to belabor the point of the importance of exercises. But to improve your brain, increase waste clearance by way of glymphatic activity and have peak cardiovascular health. But the other thing is keeping yourself hydrated to the good value of lymphatic (non-brain) and glymphatic (brain) acuity in your body. It's also crucial to memory and learning and will help you reduce neurological disorders like Alzheimer's or Parkinson's and have more energy through the day to tackle more work.

6.2 Summary:

The single best way to detox your brain is to eat right, avoid substances, and most importantly, sleep 7-9 hours per night. After you are reading this book, it's highly advised to watch the Ted Conference by renowned UC Berkeley psychologist and sleep Guru Professor Matt Walker. He gives astonishing insight to just how extraordinarily important your sleep is to the entirety of your health. As he says in his video conferences, sleep is truly your superpower, and it also is the first thing in the morning that will spearhead you forward to changing your mind.

Chapter 7: A List of Advanced Mindfulness and Meditation Techniques

Eastern traditions have practiced meditation for thousands of years. From Chinese Qigong meditation. To The Japanese "Zen." Or the Indian Dhyana form. This book will cover the Indian form and term. The word 'meditation' derives from practices to focus the mind and body together, in a way to bring inner peace and well-being. Some practices are about sensation, others breathing, or sound, an image that is held in the mind. Another form is a mantra, is a rebated prose or word which is the signature part of what is called transcendental meditation.

The Guru of T.M. was Maharishi Mahesh Yogi, who was a global meditation teacher in Jabalpur, India. In 1959, he traveled around the world to teach meditation. For some mediation is kind of shrouded in mystery as the equivalence of religion or whatnot. Rather is just teaching about relaxation and focusing. His teachings are taught all over the world. A prime example of Mindfulness-based meditation would be in the late flower power era of the 1960s, The Beatles met him in Rishikesh, India, and some of their greatest work was inspired by the trip—-including lots of The White Album was written there. The Quiet Beatle, George Harrison, was in particular captivated by him after his many years of interest in meditation—-perhaps as a way to cope with the pressure and anxiety of being in a world-famous band when his personality was more reserved. The teaching was to practice inner calmness and enlightenment. This means these ancient teachings could help one develop a new idea they never thought they'd tap into.

Maharishi, now deceased in 2008, was a man who practiced Transcendental Meditation. If you put the name The Beatles and then some Indian spiritual teacher with a long usual name, you may think this is some pretty outlandish stuff going on. But it is reality… it's just about practicing a peaceful mind with things that are stressing you out. There are various ways to do meditation, some are slightly more complex, but for a beginner, just practicing the very basics of just mindfulness—-which is just a term for focusing your attention on something without being distracted. That is something that comes into play with learning but also relaxation to cope with the abundance of stress and distractions in life. Though this will avoid some of the more religious-sounding stuff, that can be found in his 1994 book Maharishi Vedic University, which may or may not be your cup of tea. For accessible sake, we will just keep this to the bare essentials that anybody can do. The practice calms you and in the same breath, will help you learn and focus. The practices help to just get rid of stress and how to develop a greater focus on whatever they want to do in life. Here are some benefactions of meditation:

Improves Inner Peace And Psychical Health -- There is a laundry list of reasons why one should practice meditation. First and foremost, it can improve your happiness. It simply makes it so you are attuned with the world and find more solace in simple pleasures. It takes the stresses of the whole world down a couple of notches, and you can find more pleasure in casual activities. It also helps you deal with conflict, and when you get a bad hand in cards in life, things in life are not working in your favor.

As the mind and the body are connected, and because of that thing built into us called the Flight-And-Fight response, your psychic health can improve too. Once you can convince yourself that giving a less-than-perfect score on something isn't exactly like having a teeming band of lions chasing you in the forest, then your old body relaxes, and you can lower your blood pressure, which will have to reduce pain and make your sleep better and improve gastrointestinal difficulties. The mind and the body connect, and simply finding peace in your mind when your chips are down, you can improve your body. Other things mindful is said to improve:

- Improve cognition
- Improves concentration
- Improves memory
- Improves resultants
- Antidote for stress
- Lowers fatigue
- Lowers anxiety
- Lowers symptoms of asthma in kids and adolescents
- Lowers hypertension
- Lowers aggressive disposition of males
- Lowers migraine symptoms

NOTE: According to the National Institutes of Health, the scientific studies on this have not been rigorous— but from this author's perspective: it will help you relax and sleep. Knowing the above chapter's scientifically proven data of how important sleep is to one's personal health to avoid degenerative diseases is reason enough to do it.

However, according to a Harvard study, some actual scientific data proves that it does help relieve depression. 16.1 million Americans in 2015 reported having signs of depression in the last 365 days. Massachusetts General Hospital did a study on mediation on the bay using MRIs on the brain to see the changes over eight eights of mindfulness in a 'stress reduction course/" What they found is when examining the brain using an MRI. They focused on the amygdala of the brain, which is an almond-shaped cluster of cells. It also is the fearful and threatening stimuli. It also controls the brain's emotions, and especially fear-related snap judgment made decisions. Researchers saw after eight weeks the people's amygdala was 'less activated' after mindfulness. Which is the raw data: you want to relax your amygdala, and practice meditation.

7. 1 The Data On How Widely Used Is Meditation

From a 2017 study, the number of people that did any form of meditation, from mantra or mindfulness, tripled in the five years starting in 2012. It increased from 4.1 of Americans to 14.2 percent. That's a staggering increase of people more interested in releasing tension from one's life. Over the years, meditative schools are becoming popular. In the same study, 1.9 percent of 34,525 people reported they practiced mindfulness in the last year. Among others who did mindfulness, 73% did it for their overall health and to prevent diseases. The biggest number, 93%, said they did it just to mitigate stress. Half of the ones surfed, it was to sleep better at night. The other thing to take into account, smartphone growth has made mediation extremely simple. One, in particular, an app named CALM, is a meditation and breathing app that has four million subscribers. In 2017, Apple awarded Calm the App-of-the-Year of award. So this practice is becoming extremely more mainstream thanks to the influx of technology and meditation schooling.

There are many different styles of meditation and transcendental meditation. But here is a basic meditation form of Yoga of just relaxing. This is called Anapanasati or by the common tongue "Meditation breathing." Let's begin with something simple that doesn't use any mantra and is just about breathing.

7.2 Steps for Different Types of Meditation

Beginner Meditation Breathe

1. Find a Quiet Place and Get Comfortable

Located in a quiet place with no distractions. No dogs. No cats. Or children. Just you and your peace of mind. For a more modern twist to this, you get mediation apps in App Stores. The author recommends Calm, which has various styles and also calm and soothing (and intentionally boring) sleep stories for people with episodes of insomnia. Another one cuts down on non-controllable noise within or outside your bedroom, you could find noise-canceling headphones or high-end earbuds like AirPod Pro. By way of the newer technology called Noise-Canceling, many newer ones can cancel out virtually all sound and can be a revelation for people who want calm.

2. Sit Down Somewhere

For some people or nimble, you could be cross-legged but for people not, just sit straight with good posture. You could do this even in an office chair. though some like to meditate laying down somewhere. Whatever you prefer.

3. Relax Your Mind

Calm your mind and clear your mind of distractions. Then close your eyes and set a timer for 5 minutes. Clear your mind of worries and start taking a few deep but natural breaths through your nose and then through your mouth. However, it's not any icon-clad rule; breathe what feels comfortable. Then let the breath be felt through your stomach and do this for 5 minutes.

4. Focus On Your Breathing

Focus on how you are breathing and how it feels when you inhale and exhale. What that does is it blocks your consciousness from focusing on stressful things or distractions. Think of joy around you and inner peace to lower your blood pressure and just help you decompress for five minutes.

5. Refocus Thoughts

When first doing this, or when in a high-stress period in life, it can be challenging to just think of little to nothing. But focusing on your breath, or something on your body that might be tingling or whatnot will remove the cleansing of your thoughts. Rather like how some of the chapters bring up ways to cleanse your brain through sleep, and food, this cleans out your concourses of nagging the trifle of worries and stress you may have.

6. Put In The Work to Practice Often

Like many things in life, it may take a bit of time to get good at it. Michael Jordan didn't make the high school basketball team on the first try, and meditation takes a bit of practice too. But this is pretty entry-level mediation to just find a quiet place and just compress. There are various smart watches and whatnot, Apple Watch, that can ding you when your heart rate is unusually high, and then you can practice a breathing technique within an app. Just be vigilant to do some type of reacting station techniques to help lower blood pressure, sleep better (crucial), decrease stress, and help you regain focus on whatever you want to accomplish in life.

Intermediate "4-7-8 Breathing Technique".

This is another stress antidote. However, the breathing style is slightly (really) more complex as it requires counting, which is the main distinguishing factor from the aforementioned. Other than that, it's the same thing. Some doctors recommend doing this twice a day, but if that is too much, try a good quiet time to do it around mid-day when things are most stressful. Essentially, you do the same thing as above, except with this

- Inhale and breathe within your nose for two seconds
- Hold your breath for 3 seconds
- Release your breath through your nose for 4 seconds with a whoosh sound

Do this for five minutes. The exact second count is not that big of a deal, just stick to a count and use the above as a guide. If you have difficulty holding your breath, just do what feels most relaxing. It's that simple.

Advanced (Slightly More) "Universe" Meditation

This is a practice that is more advanced than the Maharishi Mahesh Yogi realm and involves a 'mantra' or, in simple terms, a repeated phrase. Sometimes when you meditate, you have to mix it up a little bit, or you become less focused to be mindful. It also might not be many people's cup of tea. But within a growth mindset, taught in this book, it could be open to different things, and learning about consciousness is just another feather in one's cap of learning. This is about shifting yourself to being "in the universe" and then having the thought of "the universe being in us."

1. Find a Quiet Place and Get Comfortable

Just like the previous, you do the same thing. Find a place, inside your house, outside in a park, where you can sit, and it's quiet.

2. Sit Down Somewhere

The same thing, sit down. Cross-legged if you can. If you are less flexible or very tall, just sit somewhere comfortable (lay down)

3. Relax, Imagine And Whisper

Form a blockade in your psyche for negative thoughts and close your eyes. Then repeat this stuff to yourself in a whisper, "I am not in the mind, the mine is in me." Then imagine a bubble of your expanding consciousness that covers your head. Feel it grow within you and repeat that.

Imagine this bubble over your body and then repeat in a whisper, "I am not in the body, the body is in me."
Then repeat, "I am not in this room, the room is in me."
As your consciousness figuratively expands around the building mutter,

"I am not in this building, the building is me."
It's here where I think you may have a point.
"I am not in this city, the city is in me."
Then.
"I am not in this country, the country is in me."
Then.
"I am not in this world, this world is in me."
Then,
"I am not in this universe, this universe is with me."

As one can see, which originally sounded kind of New Age and far-fetched Indian Mediation, one can kind of get an understanding of what this is doing: it takes your mind out of your current trials and tribulations of life to de-stress and take your mind elsewhere—even thc outer cosmo and the furthest reaches of the known or unknown galaxy.

7. 3 Summary:

Meditation has its roots in Buddhism, but you don't need to have a budget to do it. Even such athletes as LeBron James have been known to do it during the sidelights to develop inner peace and get a sense of calm. Anybody can do it, and with a laundry list of apps available in smartphone app stores, it's easier than ever to simply learn how to create a sense of tranquility in the psyche to help mitigate all the stresses of this thing called life. Meditation can be utterly transformative to have a person have not just a different outlook in life but also simply feel mentally restored like they never have before.

Chapter 8: Formulating a Strategy

The 17th-century French Military mastermind Napoléon Bonaparte knew a thing or two about strategy. So brazenly inventive were the strategies that he pioneered in how the war was done. His enemies were playing checkers, and he was playing chess. Example: During the European Napoleonic Wars, in his quest to conquer Europe, he would use a diversionary tactic to attack the enemy on its flanks instead of attacking them head-on, to avoid the line of cannon. Meaning a blindside and then baffling them with an unorthodox strategy. He also would order his military to lure the enemy onto thin ice, encircle them, and then use cannons to destroy the ice as they fell into it. He would study up on Alexander The Great, Hannibal Barca, Julius Caesar, Gustavus Adolphus, Henri Turenne, and Frederic the Great and formulate the best methods of victory on the battlefield. Though he would get a little foolhardy and invade Russia, and after he sent in 600,000 soldiers—only 100,000 would return. He would later be imprisoned, convicted, and exiled from his country and marooned on an island when he had the world at his fingertips of his innovative strategies. However, he has his run of being a brilliant military mind, the likes of which nobody had seen. He was one of the most famous—-if not the most—skilled military tacticians in all of history. These are some good techniques that can help you succeed: but confidence and erratic behavior can lead you to your doom. The bases covered in this book on topics of expanding the mind through neuroplasticity, sleeping well, eating well, and doing all of the aforementioned things will only do so much without actually formulating a worthwhile strategy. You gotta follow through. Not just take in—-but do.

One could take an educated guess that many people reading this book are bringing about a new career strategy. This brings up an important aspect of How To Change Your Mind, strategic planning. These are skill sets that are some of the most coveted skills you can have in the job marketplace. Being a person who has critical thinking skills, and can process things logically is exactly what companies want for somebody in a management position.

So What Are Strategic Thinking Skills?

You know the basics of what this is; you are an adult. To know the finest details of this takes a bit more learning. What this can do, of course, is be able to solve complex problems, plan, and all the basics of things that they are aforementioned Napoleon did to a T. But there are outlines and definitions of exact kinds of strategic thinking. Knowing these helps one think even better in a strategic manner.

Analytical Skills - Formulating information through observation and study.

Communication Skills - Speak to people with a clear vision, and network with people who can help you support your strategy.
Problem-Solving-Skills - When the Jigsaw puzzle has many pieces, you can solve the puzzle.
Planning Skills - The ability to put forth a coherent strategy that is tethered to reality.
Management Skills - The ability to lead, inspire and guide people to further your mission and also keep people in a positive frame of mind.

With the basics of what is strategic thinking out of the way, let's get into the nitty-gritty of things that can inspire you, your workforce, or your just common everyday desire for self-improvement. Developing these skills requires the initiative to do it, a growth mindset, but also putting in the grit to do it and practice it throughout life and business.

8.1 Ways to Formulating a Strategy

1. Start With a Clear Vision

A good idea can go a long way to materialize into reality. If your ambition is to be the next Oprah Winfrey, study up on her biography and how she came to prominence. First, she worked at Baltimore's WJZ-TV as a news anchor. She used that platform to catapult her to daytime TV shows which he later used as an essential vehicle to promote her various businesses. Though all the pieces came to gather, she had a vision of what she wanted to do with her business empire with a brand for the betterment of America's women. She had a purpose of delivering goodness. From books to diets, to mentally therapeutic shows, he had the plan to deliver goodness to her audience and make them feel better with tips and insight into the human condition. It's unclear if this came together as a devised strategy from the get-go Baltimore's WJZ-TV (unlucky), or if she just stumbled into it (likely), but it worked because she had a visionary belief herself to become the world's first African American woman billionaire. One thing you can say: she did really work hard, and it was no fluke. He was a uniquely informed woman with great ambition and anybody who strikes it big, some good luck came her way.

2. Look At Strengths and Weaknesses

Conventional wisdom is whatever your current situation is, examine your predicament and study your weaknesses. Some people have a natural proclivity toward creative endeavors. Other people are more structured, disciplined, and mathematical. Everybody has weaknesses, and learning how to play to your strengths can be the difference between success and failure.

When you can devise a strategy that plays off your most positive attributes and meditates on your weaknesses, you can have a better avenue for success. If you are a person who is weak in one era, learn to develop that bit by bit, and that could one day be your strength as a person. Formulate a way to press onward using your best ability and then incrementally and steadily improve your weaknesses. This is what all great strategy technicians play.

3. Study Trends That Can Be Utilized

Beware of the necessity of strategic transformation. Before the iPhone came out, smartphones had been around for years. In 1992, the Simon Personal Communicator was released. Which were a phone with a keyboard and a monochrome album touchscreen. Smartphones with a keyboard were trending upward each year with web browsers and simple apps. As you may guess, you can see what happened. In the early 2000s, Blackberry started to take off with a text messaging keyboard. Apple studied the marketplace and brought forth its own spin on the smartphone and brought back a more polished and multi-touch screen. They study trends and combine their various strengths in the iPad sector and Computer to create a revolutionary (but flawed first-generation) product. What one can do from this, is study steadily rising trends and see if one can bring forth something new to the equation. By it, writing a book in a popular genre where other genres are less popular (Zombie genre in a post-pandemic world, for instance) or something simple like selling shirts (like putting something on the shirt that is 'trending'). Find something that is 'catching on' and inspires you in creating or in business directions. There are ideas all over; one has to have an open mind to think about them for a surefooted strategy.

4. Communicate Goals

If you run a business, communicate to your employees better about your goals. The reason: From Harvard Business Review, 95% of employees they work for don't understand their company's strategy. The same research says that 85% of leaders spend less than one hour per month conveying what their strategy is. That leads to confusion in the company's workforce to get everybody on the same boat. If you have people around you in a similar field, communicate with them about some of your goals. One doesn't have to be any big level of ownership to communicate better too. Simply find peers and talk to them about some of your goals, and maybe you can formulate new ideas from some of the dialogue you are having with them of how you can expand your horizons to a new frontier.

5. Growth Arc and Decline

Microsoft didn't become the market leader for market share overnight. Bill Gates saw a strategy of selling Software to fenders and then using a licensing fee. Year by year, they began to take over the marketplace, and by the early 90s, with Windows 95, it was total domination. They had a strategy that cemented that lead. From Microsoft's inception on April 4, 1975, in Albuquerque, New Mexico as a tiny company, to becoming the world's richest man in 1995, it took time. On the flip side, as Apple was on the verge of bankruptcy in the 90s, they slowly crawled back with the release of the iMac, and the iPod and then changed the world with the iPhone, and then July 31, 2020, Apple became the world's biggest company. The two companies along with Saudi Aramco are neck and neck for who will be the biggest company in the world. The other thing to keep in mind, if you are starting a company, is realizing the 'peak' and then knowing most companies grandparents grew up on have diminished or are gone. In the year 1961, the top 25 companies on the Fortune 500 in 1961, there are only 6 still around. So be watchful of your company's steady rise to a peak and then becoming lackadaisical, ignoring the above market trends, and then declining and slowly diminishing.

6. Re-strategy When Needed

Throughout this book, there is a mention of a 'growth mindset,' and one must apply those to a strategy. Once you rest on your laurels, that is when you and your company go from peak to decline. Strategic planning is continuous as the market and, well, the whole world is always changing. A good example is RKO Pictures. They produced many classic movies of Hollywood's Golden Age. Including King Kong, Citizen Kane, It's a Wonderful Life, Snow White, and the Seven Dwarfs. RKO was one of the Big Five film studios of Hollywood's Golden Age, and they eventually went bankrupt and ended in 1957. The problem is many, but the biggest: is the lack of a winning strategy when 'their chips were down." One can go from the top of the world to nothing without clear sight of the road ahead and some degree of humility when things are going well. This method can be used not just for business, but also for personal growth and, well, personal development. If you do the same workout of your arms every day the body begins to learn and is unchallenged and the growth stops. So one has to be flexible, and re-strategize things in life to avoid declines in personal career growth, personal health, or even relationships.

7. Ask Strategic Questions

A lot of great ideas come from, "What happens if..." To blossom as a critical thinker, pertinent questions should be asked. Not just for business, but how you can improve yourself and your career strategy. According to the Harvard Business School course 'Disruptive Strategy" simply asking questions can bring forth opportunities if you are stuck in a predicament. It can remove the veil of ambiguity and shed the light on being enlightened to a new idea. You can ask questions about how you can position yourself in the market, new growth, where you will be in five years, or how the competition will grow in your field. There are many questions you could ask yourself related to the company you want to start or even yourself to improve. Form a dialogue with your inner mind to ask questions of 'what if' and then put forth a strategy, short-term, medium-term, long term that will lead to ultimate success.

8. Study Contrasting Ideas

Sometimes people with opposite opinions on yourself may have some good ideas there because of their life experience. With growth you can learn to change and adapt your way of thinking, and doors can open with new ventures to explore. Thinking of that devil's advocate personality that maybe they have some ideas in there, maybe not all of them, but some of them can be used. Do not be opposed to a good idea just because you didn't think of it first. A good example is CEO Steve Job, and Apple is known for building its own computers, the hardware, and the software, from the ground up so it seamlessly works with one another. From that, the software and hardware are harmonious and bring forth a better user experience as it cuts out the middleman software. Bill Gates's Microsoft is diametrically opposite. It took an approach of just licensing their software out, and third-party companies like Dell and Sony build the actual computer and they, in fact, would load the computer with their own software too, in addition to Microsoft's Windows. What that did, is cut down on the profit Microsoft earned as they were for the longest time purely a software company and also made the user experience less like a Frankenstein computer of different company's ideas. In the later 2010s, Microsoft studied Apple and how their strategy is not exactly market share, but rather... profit and of course high end-user experience. They saw the iPad as a shattering threat to their business empire and they changed course. So Microsoft now makes their own Microsoft computers now... something they have never done in their entire company history. Over decades, and seeing the massive rise of Apple, they changed their tune, looked at contrasting ideas, and learned that Steve Jobs's love for software and hardware synchronization brings forth just a better computer. That also, in the same token of breath, brings forth more profit to the company too. The moral of this story is, sometimes people who have different ideas than you... could have a better idea if you studied their insight.

9. School and Training Or Youtube Training

This is kind of a no-brainer. There are certain careers where formal training is key. Big lucrative jobs in any health field require extra training. But even for artistic careers, we don't necessarily need to spend a whole fortune of money, you could take some type of courses to learn different skills that you are not fully developed in. Another avenue to explore is what is en vogue right now among young and old: Youtube tutorials. There is Harvard education right on Youtube for free where one can learn just about anything from Neuroplasticity, and astrophysics, to how the pyramids were built by putting on stones on sleds or just about any topic to become an informed person in the field. But Youtube does not give you that stamp of approval a degree does on the resume, whereas a formal degree may be a great asset to your development as a person (and also boost self-esteem, which is a key to anything in life.) In terms of developing skills in creative fields, learning about history, research, writing, and self-care, YouTube is an impeccable resort to develop your psyche and understanding of the world.

10. Search for Ideas

Keep your eyes peeled and your ears and mind open for what your next idea can be. Sometimes imitation is a great source of finding new ideas and directions to take. But many ideas can spring out of nowhere on casual walks, reading 'out of-comfort zone books, in the bath, or maybe even watching a movie. Ideas are everywhere and can Germinate... in your subconscious and also consciousness. Where maybe you 'saw' or heard something but never really thought about it. Weeks, months, or even years down the line, you may spark a new idea by just encountering something different. Fresh ideas sometimes come from not following the beaten path but also can come from 'meditative' type states when you're just casually doing stuff.

11. WRITING DOWN YOUR GOALS

Marshall Arts icon Bruce Lee wrote himself a letter that he could become a Hollywood star. It was an affirmation to himself, he could become one. According to the Dominican University of California, People with actionable goals written down are 42% more likely to achieve them. Write down short-term goals, and write down long-term goals, but put them on paper (or digital file) and update them often with new things that are working and not working. Give yourself positive reinforcement that XY worked, and maybe XX didn't work. Writing is a good way to cement an action plan that you could formulate in reality. Have one-year dreams, next year's dreams, next year's dreams (et cetera.) Map our journey, like a hero's journey, like Frodo in Lord of the Rings heading to Mount Doom to destroy the One Ring. If you are filled with ambiguity about how to finish your goal, then you are troubled to actually do it. Follow that morning star of your goal-writing, every day, that you formulated as something tangibly realistic that you can achieve.

Marshall Arts icon Bruce Lee wrote himself a letter that he could become a Hollywood star. It was an affirmation to himself, he could become one. According to the Dominican University of California, People with actionable goals written down are 42% more likely to achieve them. Write down short-term goals, and write down long-term goals, but put them on paper (or digital file) and update them often with new things that are working and not working. Give yourself positive reinforcement that XY worked, and maybe XX didn't work. Writing is a good way to cement an action plan that you could formulate in reality. Have one-year dreams, next year's dreams, next year's dreams (et cetera.) Map our journey, like a hero's journey, like Frodo in Lord of the Rings heading to Mount Doom to destroy the One Ring. If you are filled with ambiguity about how to finish your goal, then you are troubled to actually do it. Follow that morning star of your goal-writing, every day, that you formulated as something tangibly realistic that you can achieve

12. Write Any Other Ideas Somewhere

In the modern age thanks to so much technology, there are numerous ways to forget a great idea. The answer: notes. Sometimes less great ideas you write down can suddenly become great ideas when you are in a different, more confident mood. Though this author is a writer and naturally writes ideas, using that technique for even working as a manager, where your eyes are open for flaws, you can write down a fix so you never forget. Depending on your field of study, this may do nothing for that career. But for other improvements in life, fixing character flaws, and writing down ideas is a good strategy.

13. Envision Your Idealized Self

If you are feeling dissolution, try this: visualize. In the occipital lobe is the visual cortex and which is a key part of the brain to use.

How? Well, If you want to become a big alpha dog CEO, rich, liked, with tons of communicating skills—-it starts with imagination, you can. Forming an inner belief in yourself that you do something by seeing yourself as that, will help crystalize it into reality. If you are filled with woe is me, I'm not good enough, and never will be good enough i.e., fixed mindset, then you are in a world of trouble. Another thing to consider, which there are many mentions of, is a thing called a vision board. Which is a collage of images cut out of a magazine or articles, printed out, and pasted on cardboard to represent your idealization self. The way you can see that board and visualize it. If you want to be a published writer, for instance, visualize yourself as one that you could be if you put in the effort, research, and action plan. Essentially that is: mental rehearsal for actually achieving it. Just remember to take into account the above-named parts about dream killing failure and reacting to it accordingly for this mental rehearsal.

14. Develop an Exponential Mindset

Short term, people overestimate what they can do. Long term, they underestimate what they can do. Growth takes gradual and steady improvements and overnight success, focusing on what's important for growth and ignoring the rest. To believe in change, block out distinctions, and look at your growth as a person/company over a longer arc than short-period gains. It is to think of oneself a bit like a stock, where yes there are times when things plummet, but over the course of many years, the growth is there. Example: the total Dow Jones stock market value on January 1st, 1962 was 724.71. Flash forward 50 years to January 1st, 2022, and it's at 36,585.06. In a nutshell, it comes down to incremental thinking of small steady moves, factoring in failure, and the instant of some overnight Powerball Lottery winning success. The former is more likely and achievable.

15. Early Bird Is First to the Worm

 American polymath and founding father, Benjamin Franklin was a quintessential early riser and planned his day by getting up at 5 a.m. That gave him ample time to be a polymath personality to pursue things like science, writing, inventing, and philosophizing. If everybody in your freelancer field is starting their day at 8 am, but you are at 11 AM, that gives your competition an advantage. Start your day early or, in a normal time frame. Ultra-successful people get a leg up on the combination by just starting their day sooner. Other benefits are less traffic, and you can have simple 'me time to take in information from the previous day to formulate a plan that day. There are strong benefits to early rising but, as you may remember from the previous chapter, not at the expense of getting proper sleep. So if you wanna be an early riser make sure you go to bed at a proper time and make sure you have a full restorative sleep during that time.

16. Innovate When You Can

It takes a long of brazen audacity to do something that is how of the box thinking. All great inventions come from that mental framework of doing something different. Serbian-American futuristic and pioneering inventor, Nikola Tesla invented the alternating current from the time-tested 'direct current.' All breakouts are about thinking a bit differently from the herd. Another example is Amazon, where in the mid-90s, there were no online booksellers to pick up your copy of Jurassic Park. So Jeff Bezos created that and, bit by bit, using many of the above techniques, saw steady improvement in the innovative idea of an online marketplace. The reality is many people are in a fixed mindset, and if you adopt a growth mindset and then look to innovate, you can devise a unique strategy for innovation. Just don't put all your chickens in one basket, have a fallback plan on said innovation, and think of ways to overcome if something doesn't take off immediately. Another more recent example would be From that historical blunder of this, Japanese video game titan Nintendo. In 2012 they rereleased their least successful home console ever: the polarizing and misunderstood Wii U. Which was a video game system with an unwieldy tablet-like screen that looked unsightly. They wanted mobile and home but at the same time. Nintendo was in dire straits, and its stock and market share were decimated from its previous ultra-successful Wii system. What they did: they learned from failure and made a system, the Switch, that is a home console to play on the tv and then gets taken out of the dock to be played on the go. Nintendo learned from its failures with the Wii U, reworked it, make it more accessible, devised a straightforward name, and created most likely their most successful console of all time in terms of sales. Failure and re-strategizing can bring about innovation and unheard success.

8.2 Summary

One does not need to be the world chess champion Magnus Carlsen being good at strategy. Many people in life don't formulate any kind of strategy and are moving through life like a leaf in the wind. Devising a strategy for your life, career, and love life, and making sure it is realistic, thoughtful, and able to adapt to changes, is key to achieving what you want. Just don't use these time-tested strategies to conquer Europe like Napoleon Bonaparte or anything.

Chapter 9: Wandering Mind - DMN/TPN Mode, and How To Switch

Famed Psychiatrist Sigmund Freud taught about how the dynamic subconscious can affect our day-to-day lives. He studies various therapeutic techniques of how things we aren't thinking about control our day-to-day lives. He revolutionized psychiatry by studying the subconscious and Psychoanalysis. We hear that studying is the part where we are shut off to introspection, and our brain is kind of on autopilot. Everybody daydreams. When you are sitting at work thinking about that trip to Venice Beach California. Or that time you fell in love with somebody you shouldn't have. Or simple pleasures like a French Silk Pie. Or maybe you have Chronomentrophobia, a fear of clocks and or the more common fear of time itself. Whatever is glowing in your brain during the day. But sometimes non-commandeered thoughts can affect you from being productive in life and....happiness. One must have the presence in mind when to turn the switch to OFF. First, from various research in 2001 by scientist Marcus Raichle, M.D, let's learn the distinctions between DMN and PTN.

What Is DMN (Default Mode Network)?

This is layman's terms: a time with the brain is resting and controlling high-order functions. A more medical explanation: This is a part of the brain that is a loose connection with neurons and spontaneously reacts to various areas of the brain in 'passive moments.'. Let's first explain a bit about the interworking of the brain and how much it encompasses. The part of the brain that has DMN temporal lobe, prefrontal cortex, the posterior cingulate cortex. All of these are parts of the brain that are in charge of memory (prefrontal), ranging emotions and thoughts towards goals (posterior cingulate), autobiographical memorization, and the ability to reflect from the posterior cingulate. In a microcosm: this part of the brain that controls various emotional states, introspection, mind-wondering, long-term memory, Attention Deficit Disorder (A.D.D.), and hyperactivity. By Sigmund Freud's definition, this would be the subconscious mind and also the preconscious mind and daydreaming.

Positive Constructive Day-Dreaming

These constant wishful thoughts like the aforementioned trip to Vegas California, or having a French Silk pie, or dreaming about being an elementary school teacher. All positive and somewhat productive thoughts swirl in one's brain. These—-in moderation—-are good to have to go in your head.

Guilty-Dysphoric Daydreaming

When your brain is full of tempestuous rumination thoughts in your head. Negative Nancy. Woe is me. The pessimist. Or maybe something serious is going on, like Post Traumatic Stress Disorder from serving. The counterproductive thoughts that bog down your day, like being stuck in wet cement.

Poor Attention Control Daydreaming

 This is when you have a hard time concentrating on work, and your mind is filled with a random, sometimes fragmented web of thoughts. This affects your work, communication skills, and happiness. It is equally bad as the above one and may require meditation and/or medication.

What Is a Task-positive Network (TPN)?

This is part of the brain related to focus and would be tied closely to Sigmund Freud's conscious mind. We are actively doing something and keenly aware of it, like, well, writing a book on TPN, for instance. You are actively playing basketball. Or within a conversation with a co-worker. It's where you need razor-like concentration and then uses short-term memory to make snap decisions. Within your mode of consciousness, you are happier than if you are just 'there' like the above. Distinguishing these two methods of thought is important to know how to regulate your emotions and your behavior.

The Underlying Problem:

The two modes of thought are at odds with one another, like Dr. Jekyll or Mr. Hyde. When one is active, the other is less active. If you don't have a present to mind to know when you are DMN parts of the brain can creep in like a wandering toddler. It also hinders you from living a balanced and productive life where your subconscious is starting to rule you. According to research from American psychologist Richard J. Davidson, the average American spends 47% of the time not paying attention to what they are doing. A wandering daydreaming mind could use a lasso to reign in so you can be more productive and more balanced. Studies have found there to be a link between DMN mode and depression and that meditation to get the brain to get out of that thinking pattern, can snap one out of Default Mode Activity of depressing daydreams of lack of concentration. The person's default mode of their brain is about various factors, nature (DNA) vs. nurture (how they learned to cope), and every person, just like the unique contours of their face, is different. So the best answer is to be aware of your DMN, how you respond to your feelings, and learn methods to the brain from depressing or counter-productive thought patterns that spiral down like a kamikaze pilot. People who sticker with chronic depression would especially be beneficial from meditation to augment their thinking patterns for their welfare. The problem with daydreamers and writers having a natural skill is that it is tied to both depression and creativity. Over the course of time, researchers have found three types of daydreamers. And the types of daydreams from when the brain is in DMN are a lot like Dr. Jekyll and Mr. Hyde of the brain.

Correlation Between DMN and Empathy

Understanding emotions is critical in understanding social situations. Understanding social cues, body language, minor changes in voice, reading faces, and just the indirectness of some social interventions is important. There have been various clinical studies using fMRI machines to determine a greater understanding of our minds. Our cognitive empathy part of our brain connects and overlaps with the Default Mode Network of the brain. This means if you are an overzealous DMN, be it from depression, injury, or neurological disorder, in your brain, your perception of others may be thrown askew. The simple understanding: your brain is more focused on itself, like narcissism, than it is on others' feelings. As various meditation gurus would say: you're simply not 'not present.' Now there is a Scientific Neuroimaging understanding of what exactly they're not present in. To have your empathy firing on all cylinders and you are fully reading people and connecting to people, one has to understand when to put their grips on that DMN in the brain or you will have a social disconnection from your peers. If you want to connect better and be that social butterfly, put a lasso on that DMN.

Default Mode Network and Neurological Disorders

If you are not controlling this part of your brain, you can exacerbate negative feelings. First, you are susceptible to developing severe depression and then hyperactivity and have bipolar disorder and PTSD (Post Traumatic Stress Disorder).

Learn to control your DMN to thwart or reduce the chances of many neurological disorders. Having an out-of-balance DMN is tied to many white matter abnormalities and neuropsychiatric disorders. Various studies and neuroimaging found information on the following neurodevelopmental disorders:

Attention Deficit Hyperactivity Disorder (ADHD)

Research has shown that people with ADHD have less DMN connection in the brain. There is a decreased activity where the brain is a DMN. It also causes negative effects on the ability of self-reflection for a long period of time.

Autism (ASD)

The same can be said with people with autism and understanding social cues, there is a correlation between the two and their effects on DMN within the resting state.

PTSD (Post Traumatic Stress Disorder)

Finally, clinical studies of PTSD also have abnormalities in the brain in the DMN. There has been a severe change in what is going on in the Brain chemistry during DMN. The effects of DMN on people who are mentally scared with PTSD are striking.

Chronic Pain

People with chronic pain show they have high DMN activity in the brain. The pain modulatory system systems are, understandably, highly active, and that ties into the DMN network, where they are mentally 'checking out.'

Schizophrenia

Clinically research showed that people with Schizophrenia are more active with DMN. Meaning their 'restful' state of the brain is more out of balance and thus controlling the person. When there are tasks that require attention, the DMN is unusually active. When that is reduced, TPN (when the brain focuses) does reduce the DMN. Also, other neurological disorders in people with schizophrenia is paranoia, and they also have high DMN while they are actively trying to have razor-like focus using TPN.

Alzheimer's Disease

Most people know what this is, the reduction of the brain acting by way of toxic beta-amyloid 42 plagues build up. What these plagues do is collect between neurons in your brain. The result: they disrupt cell function and affect memory and motor skills. But what has been discovered through clinical research, is the reduction of brain acuity goes into the Default Mode Network too. Antecedent factors, meaning—-what is triggering, appear to be negative balanced DMN that appears to be the first steps to having this neurodegeneration in the brain. If you want to keep your brain avoiding this, be mindful of abnormalities in your DMN.

9.1 Tips on How To Switch How Out of DMN

The first step is recognizing you may have a problem with 'not being present and DMN. What you can do is try rote learning, which is a repetitive behavior that forges is deeply embedded learning. It is a memorization technique for doing the same thing again and again. There are many things one can do to lessen the consequences of having an overactive DMN mode. Each time you are within DMN and your mind is in la-la land, and you understand it, implement steps and habitual patterns to switch out of it each time. Do not stay locked in your head but rather in action to control your mind rambunctious mind with these steps

Stay Motivated

If you have a profession doing highly repetitive work, try to find something you can do for many hours that stimulates your mind. Doing the same thing every day, be it cleaning floors, or changing light bulbs, doesn't use much cognitive function and puts you into a DMN and just zone out it's the Alpha Centauri galaxy. Seek mentally stimulating things around people or changing work that you can interact with, not just be sucked into the Twilight Zone of television.

Meditation

Rigorous methods have found that practicing mindfulness and meditation can lessen the effects of DMN overpowering your day-to-day life. It's worth noting that T.M. or Transcendental Medication, in particular, can reduce the negative neurological consequences of DMN. From Zen to Mindfulness to Qigong, anything meditation will help.

Acupuncture

Brain Imaging with fMRI (Functional magnetic resonance imaging) has found that the ancient method of needles into the skin can help alleviate distracting DMN thoughts. It distracts you with minor pain across the body, so you are focused on the here and now for long periods. Throughout many sessions, you could have positive results.

Medication

Taking some type of meditation for focusing, like Citalopram, Escitalopram, and Fluoxetine can help with regaining focus and reducing that out-of-alignment DMN. Ketamine, in particular, disturbs the frontal lobe DMN, which will help other parts of the brain control get out of the stranglehold of subconscious control.

Psychedelics

Over the years, magic mushrooms have proven to have many health benefits besides listening to Pink Floyd's Dark Side of The Moon. The National Library of Medicine did a study on Hallucinogenic mushrooms called psilocybin and LSD on the brain. These types of psychedelics have been used for centuries in healing. They found that it reduces the lesser the connections of DMN by way of temporally "ego-dissolution" by losing the senses when using these substances and creating changes in personality. Essentially, what happens when taking Magic Mushroom: the brain becomes more interconnected. They also found this method is good for people with depression and other neurological disorders.

9.2 Summary

One does not need to be exactly Sigmund Freud to understand how the subconscious will affect your consciousness—-for good or ill. These are various techniques to Shepard focus in your life and also have a presence of mind of your DMN. Having at least a basic understanding of how DMN and TPN form the various interacting brain regions for good or bad. Make changes to your self-awareness within yourself to be on the first step for a powerful transformation of who you can be. How you handle your DMN can leave a lasting impact of who you are... or will become. The key to unlocking being locked in your mind is being aware of it.

Chapter 10: ADHD - Deep Look Into the ADHD Brain in Children and Adults

If you are a person with a wandering mind, restless, can't concentrate for long periods, and a bit unruly when forced to be confined, that is a tall tale sign of ADHD. Or, in non-acronym terms: attention deficit hyperactivity disorder. If you are a person who has this—well—- you are not alone.

The facts: there are 3 million cases in the United States cases per year with ADHD. The list of truly exceptional people is quite staggering. Including record-winning gold medal list Olympian Michael Phelps. So does comedian Howie Mandel from America's Got Talent. So does 2016 gymnastic gold medallist Simone Biles. Hip-hop/producer Black Eyed Peas member will.i.am. Renowned political analyst James Carville. In just about every field you can imagine, people can have ADHD, and also the same token, breathing excels in life.

Many people grow out of adulthood, but some people still have it as they get older. 8.4 percent of kids and 2.5% of adults have attention deficit disorder. Within the United States, it is estimated that 6.4 kids between the ages of four and seventeen have been diagnosed with affliction. Within the western parts of the United States are the lowest cases, the Scientific reason for that is unclear but could be a contributor to the weather. Within the coldest region of the country, the Midwest is more prevalent where many states are unusually high compared to others. This could mean, from this writer's perspective, there could be some correlation between the two. Kentucky has the highest rate at 14.8% of kids. While the lowest rate, just so happens to be the hottest state with Nevada at 4.2%. Other states are California at 5.9% and Arkansas, Louisiana, and Indiana, all around 14.6% and 13.3%. But generally, midwestern states are hit the heaviest with this problem with kids. If you are from these necks of the woods, and you have a hard time focusing and are restless, you may have ADHD. Nevertheless, this disorder is an epidemic of proportions in certain regions of the country and affects people's entire lives.

10.1 So What Is ADHD?

Well, it's the difficulty concentrating, essentially, and acting impulsive. Adults with this affliction may have low self-esteem and hypersensitivity to criticism. If you are a person who can't still, fidgets, and your mind is in dreamland a lot in the aforementioned DMN, that is a good example of what ADHD is. The problems are not from being defiant and not generally about the person understanding the directions given either. And if you are a person with ADHD, here's some rocket fuel motivation that you can still accomplish anything you put your mind to: according to Michael Phelps, the winner of the most gold medals in Olympic history, his teachers told him, "I had a teacher tell me that I would never amount to anything and I would never be successful."

Those sometimes tough love could motivate a kid, that teacher's brutal assessment of him was completely off the mark and uncalled for. So what gets into the medical understanding of what precisely is ADHD.

The three types of neurobehavioral disorders for ADHD are:

Predominantly inattentive presentation - This is when you have difficulty concentrating or can't sustain attention, procrastinate, and just have general forgetfulness. Has difficulty completing work and mind wonders, and they misplace things.

Predominantly hyperactive/impulsive presentation - This is about the movement of your body and just being hyperactive. Restlessness, fidgeting, talking too much, and just being impulsive decisions.

Combined presentation.
This is when you have all of the symptoms combined.

Other things to consider not ADHD:

(ODD) Oppositional Defiant Disorder - This is behavior rider when a child is unruly, and defiant, and harbors hostility towards peers, teachers, and in particular, people within the authority. It is a personality trait of being rebellious.

Autism Disorder

You owe your child to being on the spectrum of an autism disorder which prevents you from socially interacting, learning, and an assortment of other things.

Diagnosis

To adequately determine if you or your child have ADHD, the symptoms need to persist for six months or more. The way it is determined if you or your child have it would be an assessment with a questionnaire by a child or adult psychiatrist. This would involve a series of interview questions and personal reports from other people that encountered the patient. Another thing that would happen to diagnose ADHD, to determine there isn't anything else medically abnormal, is a physical examination by a doctor. The reason why it is cortical to have a physical examination to rule out if there is substance abuse is proven, anxiety, head injury, substance abuse or thyroid issue, neurological mood disorder, or the above (ODD) Oppositional

Defiant Disorder. Or an fMRI could be done on the brain to understand the abnormality in the behavior.

Causes for ADHD

There has been scientific evidence that your very genetics comes into play for underlying causes of ADHD, not just environmental factors such as a chaotic household. But geneticists have not determined what the gene combination is that is the catalyst for the neurological disorder. Using a magnetic field and radio frequencies of MRI of the brain, they have found anatomical differences in reduced gray area and white matter between the brains of children with ADHD and those without. They have also found through brain imaging that the front lobes, caudate nucleus, and cerebellar vermis are different from people with ADHD. Other things that come into play are the child's birth weight, and being born prematurely. Other underlying factors of having toxins in utero such as smoking, lead, or alcohol and the mother having an exorbitant amount of stress while pregnant. 10.2 Ways to Improve From ADHD

1. Medication

There are various treatments for ADHD, from therapy to psychiatric intervention. The first approach is the medication one could take, such as Ridellan. Talking to your physician is best to determine if medication is the best treatment for ADHD or if something like behavior therapy or both is more beneficial. These can help relieve symptoms of ADHD to help the stranglehold it has day to day life. The five types of psychostimulant medication for ADHD are:

Ritalin - AKA methylphenidate
Vyvanse - AKA lisdexamfetaminc
Monograph - AKA dexamfetamine

Strattera- AKA atomoxetine

Intuniv- AKA guanfacine

All of these medications have side effects like drowsiness, headaches, vomiting, and diarrhea. Ones like Ritalin have a rapid heartbeat, panic, and could cause heart failure. Consult your doctor on all of these to determine if this is the best route to treat you or your child's ADHD.

Behavior Therapy

According to research from the National Institute of Mental Health, they have found that medication and addition to behavior therapy are the best way to treat ADHD. This study was also reinforced by the American Academy of Pediatrics on the power of the two combination methods. Consult a board-certified physician and a psychiatrist on this method to perhaps make life-changing changes in yourself or your children. These are some Cognitive Behavioral Therapy (CBT) tips from the According to the director Center for Children and Families at UONY William Pelham, Jr., Ph.D., Marsha Linehan, Ph.D., ABPP, a professor of psychology at the University of Washington, Carol Brady, Ph.D., a child psychologist practicing in Houston. The reason is enough for this: a clinical study by Boston's Massachusetts General Hospital, conducted in 2010, found the combination of the two methods brings about the best results.

Therapy #1 - Children: Positive/Negative Reinforcement

Formulate a strategy to control your child's behavior through positive and negative reinforcement. First, devise a reward system for your kid for exemplary behavior. On the flip side, they are dismayed by negative behavior by ignoring it so they don't get attention. The kid might just be acting out to get attention. Snatch away things, such as video games or smartphones, if negative behavior spirals downward. If you find something that causes the unruly behavior, restrict it from the child.

Therapy #2 - Adults: Control DMN/Daydreaming Thoughts

Controlling negative pattern thinking from the subconscious. The DMN, the part of your brain on autopilot, is something that can be controlled to help with ADHD. If your mind is stuck in a loop-a-loop of negative thoughts, then control them by being mindful of them. For some of the more severe issues like hyperactivity, negative pattern thinking, and being impulsive, these techniques won't be 100% a remedy but lessens their impact on them. According to research, there is no evidence that CBT can replace psychostimulant drug therapy, but evidence of these techniques with a combination of a daily capsule can bring about lowering the symptoms.

CHANGE DEFAULT MINDSET TO LESSEN THE IMPACT OF ADHD

Overgeneralization - If you make one mistake, you see it as a pattern and overreact emotionally. One is too hard on oneself for minor human error.

Comparative Thinking - Comparing yourself against unrealistic expectations of others, then feeling inferior. If you are not as good as the greatest, then you are not good at all methods of thinking.

Mind Reading - Believe in you have the ability to clairvoyance. You see people and think the worst they are thinking in reality, their thoughts are more mundane.

Fortune telling - prophecies that things are always turned on badly. The result: it can become a self-fulfilling prophecy because of that.

All-Or-Nothing thinking - This is when you see the totality of everything in extremes of black and white. There is no middle ground. All things are good and bad.

Magnification And Minimization - Believing seller accomplishments in life as minor but believing the minor failures as colossal mistakes.

"Should" statements - Being stubborn, not flexible to have things your own way, which opens the doors for self-criticism and feelings of bitterness.

Therapy #3 - Adults Dialectical Behavior Therapy

Neuro-psychology can be mitigated using Dialectical Behavioral Therapy (DBT). This involves going to weekly support group sessions to develop better-coping skills in social situations. This talk therapy can help improve personality disorders or how you handle interpersonal conflicts. It can be used to lessen mood disorders and self-harm, and suicidal thoughts. DBT can be taught to offer support to those who are struggling in society with personality issues that hold them back and may bring the arm to themselves. It uses various methods like mindfulness and acceptance of oneself and improving self-esteem.

Therapy #4 - Coaching

There are so many aspects in life to learn and a professionally trained coach can help one learn how to handle things better. What are coaches for time management, planning, motivation, being balanced, and making healthy decisions—-is endless. Having a Guiding Light coach person in your life who can support you through thick and thin and a huge way to build self-esteem and learn to modify behavior. There are ones for adults and children who can guide them along through dark passes in life or just give them simple pointers on how to handle situations that may arise.

Therapy #5 - Neurofeedback

This is not the pin eyeballs open and forced to watch the movie "The Ludovico Technique" featured in the Stanley Kubrick movie The Clockwork Orange. Rather than putting something on your head. This is Neurotherapy that uses devices strapped to give biofeedback through an electrode on the head. This is used for impulse control to get them to change their method- of thinking. This can help people from being unruly and help tame their aggressive and counterproductive personality traits. The jury is still out on clinical research if this works or not.

Therapy #6 - Play Therapy

This method is simply being playful with your children to get them to relax, bond with them, reduce anxiety and improve self-esteem. Many children, perhaps the middle child, can somewhat feel left out if there is somebody born after them or before them. (Research the middle child syndrome.) For your child to feel hopeful, happy, and with self-esteem, they must play and also bond with their parents through playtime. So if you get left alone a lot and have problems in school, maybe it's time to bond with them more and play some Nintendo or pick-up basketball with them.

Therapy #7 - Music Therapy

Music does a lot more than just getting your head to bob up and down through a stimulating melody—the psychological effects also help focus, be hyper, and develop social skills and memory. This helps with cognitive ability and helps produce neurons for neuroplasticity. It also brings pleasure which helps the pleasure hormone, dopamine, rise in the brain. Other things music can do is reduce anxiety, and blood pressure would assist a person to relax, learn and be a more socially skilled member of society. "Listen For Life" founder Donna Stoering gave a Ted Conference about how beneficial music is to regulating emotions, helping to sleep, and especially beneficially for somebody with hyperactivity disorder: calming rage. Finally, a clinic done in 2020 found Music therapy improves attentiveness in children.

Therapy #8 - Art Therapy

There is this thing called Right Brain Left Brain and Its Relevance to Art. Which means the left brain is more into math and language. The right brain is more art. Some children, and adults, are simply more right-brain dominant thinkers and that is what they are interested in. Meanwhile, many things in life are not art in the slightest, and their minds wander. The solution: Doing anything artistic to help focus concentration. If you have a passion for your project, then your focus only increases exponentially. That is why creating art can help a child or an adult hone their focusing skills. In your wandering mind, children are taught to give razor-like focus on things they enjoy, which can help them develop acuity for other things. Other things art does help deal with emotionally and develop a problem-solving need for everyday life.

Therapy #9 - Equine Therapy

This is one of the more esoteric ones, but there is scientific data on this treatment. Predator animals like dogs and cats hide their feelings to hint. Other prey animals, like horses and donkeys, express their feelings. National Library of Medicine, gave some input on this published study that horseback riding with 5 children helped them improve ADHD. They found that therapeutic horseback had a positive effect on their mental health; instead of simply talking to somebody about their problem, they bonded with animals. There are various activities you can do with a horse, such as Hippotherapy by using the very moment of the horse to improve mental health. Other ones are Therapeutic driving where you would just write the horse with a carriage attached to it. Though, for the everyday child, or the everyday adult, finding the horse to ride may not be realistic. But if you live on a farm somewhere and have some steeds, consider taking a gallop.

Therapy #10 - Video Game Therapy

If the last one about horsing sounds a little bit esoteric and a pipe dream treatment, this one is more realistic for most kids, and would love to hear it. In a Study at Duke by Scott Kollins, a professor in psychiatry and behavioral sciences, he found video games are not an alternative treatment for ADHD but are 'promising.' The study found that kids that took no medication and then played video games 25 minutes a week showed a huge improvement in attention scores, according to Dr. Kollins. It makes sense: video games, especially the more competitive online ones like Call of Duty, take an extraordinary amount of concentration for perhaps dozens of hours to even get adequate at.

10.3 Summary

From controlling DMN to self-help groups to medication to video games, to even riding horses, there are various forms of treatment for ADHD. These techniques and medications could help improve someone who has attention deficit disorder and live a better, more successful life. So whether you are young, old, or in between, if you're a person that struggles with concentration, now is the time to take control of that and live up to your maximum potential so you can reach the Mount Everest of happiness.

Closing Thoughts

This book was compiled through various clinical studies and articles written on the Internet to improve one's mind and outlook on life. Just like a lot of things in life, not everything is a one size fits all method. So there are certain things in this book that will work well for you and your personality, but other things may not quite be cohesive with who you are as a person.

From my personal experience as someone who works as a writer, some of the best things you could do to improve yourself are to have a lifelong love for reading, exercise, diet, and keeping a positive mentality through the trials and tribulations of life. If there is one thing in this book that you could take out there that will most transform, like a moth to a butterfly, and get you out of that turtle shell: the extraordinary and straightforward information from Dr. Carol Dweck's growth mindset versus a fixed mindset study. It is this sobering realization, that you are not fixed at birth from your intelligence and abilities, and if you are weak in an area so be it. Anything else, you can grow exponentially by creating a positive pattern and doing it every single day. Through stride and strife, overcoming hurdles with determination, you could become a better, more emotionally balanced person with incremental improvement. The mindset of personal growth is transformative, and understanding it is not exactly high-brow neuroscience either. That's the difference between progression in life, and being shackled by the iron grip of worrying about failure and slowly regressing backward to depression. As someone who has grown considerably since he got out of college, that was truly the distinguishing factor from my personal growth and a lot of my peers in my youth. Many of the people I grew up with, some white graduated high school, or even college, and kind of gave up on gradually improving on various things in their life. Understanding what person you and those around you and what kind of frame of mind they are in, will help you spearhead forward in life.

In closing, I truly wish you the best in your pursuit to expand your mind and perhaps greater, sunnier horizons through various techniques found in this book. I sincerely thank you for reading and hope these words inspired you to follow your dreams with steadfast passion through pitfalls. In the wise words of Walt Disney, "All of our dreams can come true, if we have the courage to pursue them."

RESOURCES:

INTRODUCTION

Brain plasticity. Brain Plasticity - an overview | ScienceDirect Topics. (n.d.). Retrieved October 28, 2022, from https://www.sciencedirect.com/topics/neuroscience/brain-plasticity

Encyclopædia Britannica, inc. (n.d.). Neuroplasticity. Encyclopædia Britannica. Retrieved October 28, 2022, from https://www.britannica.com/science/neuroplasticity

University, H. (2013, December 16). The 'Mozart effect' of having kids study music? it's only a myth, researchers find. The Washington Post. Retrieved October 28, 2022, from https://www.washingtonpost.com/national/health-science/the-mozart-effect-of-having-kids-study-music-its-only-a-myth-researchers-find/2013/12/13/bd2ede46-6351-11e3-a373-0f9f2d1c2b61_story.html

CHAPTER ONE

Cherry, K. (n.d.). Neuroplasticity: How experience changes the brain. Verywell Mind. Retrieved October 28, 2022, from https://www.verywellmind.com/what-is-brain-plasticity-2794886

Caverzasio, S., Amato, N., Manconi, M., Prosperetti, C., Kaelin-Lang, A., Hutchison, W. D., & Galati, S. (2017, December 24). Brain plasticity and sleep: Implication for movement disorders. Neuroscience & Biobehavioral Reviews. Retrieved October 28, 2022, from https://www.sciencedirect.com/science/article/abs/pii/S0149763417305109

Cherry, K. (n.d.). Neuroplasticity: How experience changes the brain. Verywell Mind. Retrieved October 28, 2022, from https://www.verywellmind.com/what-is-brain-plasticity-2794886

Levine, H. (2022, July 29). 5 brain exercises that Can keep your mind sharp. AARP. Retrieved October 28, 2022, from https://www.aarp.org/health/brain-health/info-2022/workouts-for-brain-health.html

Wikimedia Foundation. (2022, October 13). Neuroplasticity. Wikipedia. Retrieved October 28, 2022, from https://en.wikipedia.org/wiki/Neuroplasticity

Person. (2020, June 17). How to rewire your brain: 6 neuroplasticity exercises. Healthline. Retrieved October 28, 2022, from https://www.healthline.com/health/rewiring-your-brain#travel

Kaplan, E. (2017, December 26). How to rewire your brain for massive success, according to Neuroscience. Medium. Retrieved October 28, 2022, from https://medium.com/thrive-global/how-to-rewire-your-brain-for-massive-success-according-to-neuroscience-f051a30395d1

Mark Stibich, P. D. (2020, March 2). Top 10 ways to improve your brain fitness. Verywell Mind. Retrieved October 28, 2022, from https://www.verywellmind.com/top-ways-to-improve-your-brain-fitness-2224137

Is literacy declining?: Inside higher ed. Higher Ed Gamma. (n.d.). Retrieved October 28, 2022, from https://www.insidehighered.com/blogs/higher-ed-gamma/literacy-declining

S;, C. R. M. A. C. (n.d.). N-3 fatty acids: Role in neurogenesis and neuroplasticity. Current medicinal chemistry. Retrieved October 28, 2022, from https://pubmed.ncbi.nlm.nih.gov/23746276/

Zhang L;Luo J;Zhang M;Yao W;Ma X;Yu SY; (n.d.). Effects of curcumin on chronic, unpredictable, mild, stress-induced depressive-like behaviour and structural plasticity in the lateral amygdala of rats. The international journal of neuropsychopharmacology. Retrieved October 28, 2022, from https://pubmed.ncbi.nlm.nih.gov/24405689/

Sisson, M. (2021, August 24). 16 ways to increase neuroplasticity (and why that's important). Mark's Daily Apple. Retrieved October 28, 2022, from https://www.marksdailyapple.com/16-ways-to-increase-neuroplasticity-and-why-thats-important/

Moore, Z., Kemberling, C., Barlow, S., Saito, E., & Jeffrey Edwards, P. D. (n.d.). Effects of the ketogenic diet on learning and memory. BYU ScholarsArchive. Retrieved October 28, 2022, from https://scholarsarchive.byu.edu/library_studentposters_2021/25/

Rossi, E., Cheng, H., Kroll, J. F., Diaz, M. T., & Newman, S. D. (2017, November 21). Changes in white-matter connectivity in late Second Language Learners: Evidence from diffusion tensor imaging. Frontiers in psychology. Retrieved October 28, 2022, from
https://www.ncbi.nlm.nih.gov/pmc/articles/PMC5702476/

CHAPTER TWO

Sur, S. (2022, October 27). Winning mentality: 10 secrets to developing & maintaining it. Wealthful Mind. Retrieved October 28, 2022, from https://wealthfulmind.com/winning-mentality-secrets-to-developing-it/#:~:text=A%20winning%20mentality%20is%20a,seeks%20growth%20in%20every%20opportunity.

How to surround yourself with good people in your life. tonyrobbins.com. (n.d.). Retrieved October 28, 2022, from https://www.tonyrobbins.com/stories/business-mastery/surround-yourself-with-quality-people/

U.S. Department of Health and Human Services. (n.d.). Alcohol's damaging effects on the brain. National Institute on Alcohol Abuse and Alcoholism. Retrieved October 28, 2022, from https://pubs.niaaa.nih.gov/publications/aa63/aa63.htm

Pearson, J., Naselaris, T., Holmes, E. A., & Kosslyn, S. M. (2015, October). Mental imagery: Functional mechanisms and clinical applications. Trends in cognitive sciences. Retrieved October 28, 2022, from https://www.ncbi.nlm.nih.gov/pmc/articles/PMC4595480/

NBA. (2022, June 14). Final 4:39 of Michael Jordan's last Bulls Game vs jazz - 1998 NBA Finals. YouTube. Retrieved October 28, 2022, from https://www.youtube.com/watch?v=VlbC8q4VkL4

Wikimedia Foundation. (2022, October 28). Tom Brady. Wikipedia. Retrieved October 28, 2022, from https://en.wikipedia.org/wiki/Tom_Brady

Campbell, S. (2016, October 13). 10 ways to develop an unshakable belief in yourself. Entrepreneur. Retrieved October 28, 2022, from https://www.entrepreneur.com/living/10-ways-to-develop-an-unshakable-belief-in-yourself/283645

CHAPTER THREE

Mayo Foundation for Medical Education and Research. (2022, February 3). How to stop negative self-talk. Mayo Clinic. Retrieved October 28, 2022, from https://www.mayoclinic.org/healthy-lifestyle/stress-management/in-depth/positive-thinking/art-20043950

Mayo Foundation for Medical Education and Research. (2021, July 29). Stress relief from laughter? it's no joke. Mayo Clinic. Retrieved October 28, 2022, from https://www.mayoclinic.org/healthy-lifestyle/stress-management/in-depth/stress-relief/art-20044456

The neuroscience of breaking out of negative thinking (and ... - inc.com. (n.d.). Retrieved October 28, 2022, from https://www.inc.com/nate-klemp/try-this-neuroscience-based-technique-to-shift-your-mindset-from-negative-to-positive-in-30-scconds.html

M.D., C. B. (2021, August 17). 85% of what you worry about never happens. Medium. Retrieved October 28, 2022, from https://medium.com/mind-cafe/85-of-what-you-worry-about-never-happens-3f748aab16de

Cho, J. (2016, December 28). The science behind how Mindfulness can help break negative thought patterns. Forbes. Retrieved October 28, 2022, from https://www.forbes.com/sites/jeenacho/2016/12/27/the-science-behind-how-mindfulness-helps-you-to-break-negative-thought-patterns/?sh=68c751db4119

Team, B. and S. (2022, March 11). How to turn around your negative thinking. Cleveland Clinic. Retrieved October 28, 2022, from https://health.clevelandclinic.org/turn-around-negative-thinking/

Morris, L. (2022, March 11). 3 ways to turn negative into positive. wikiHow. Retrieved October 28, 2022, from https://www.wikihow.com/Turn-Negative-Into-Positive

Clark, D. (n.d.). 3 ways to turn negativity into positivity. TTI Success Insights Blog. Retrieved October 28, 2022, from https://blog.ttisi.com/3-ways-to-turn-negativity-into-positivity

Writer. (n.d.). When nothing's funny, even simulated laughter can be good medicine. Home. Retrieved October 28, 2022, from https://www.globallymealliance.org/blog/when-nothings-funny-even-simulated-laughter-can-be-good-medicine

Substance abuse and mental health services administration. SAMHSA. (n.d.). Retrieved October 28, 2022, from https://www.samhsa.gov/

Bradshaw, F. (2022, April 8). How to turn negative thoughts into positive actions. Mind Tools Blog. Retrieved October 28, 2022, from https://www.mindtools.com/blog/how-to-turn-negative-thoughts-into-positive-actions/

The real health benefits of smiling and laughing. The Real Health Benefits of Smiling and Laughing | SCL Health. (n.d.). Retrieved

October 28, 2022, from https://www.sclhealth.org/blog/2019/06/the-real-health-benefits-of-smiling-and-laughing/

Building Self-esteem: A Self-Help Guide, SAMHSA booklet SMA-3715. (n.d.). Building Self-Esteem by Changing Negative Thoughts. Building self-esteem by changing negative thoughts. Retrieved October 28, 2022, from https://www.mentalhelp.net/self-esteem/changing-negative-thoughts/

Santos-Longhurst, A. (2019, February 21). How to think positive and have an optimistic outlook: 8 tips. Healthline. Retrieved October 28, 2022, from https://www.healthline.com/health/how-to-think-positive#overview

https://academic.oup.com/aje/article/185/1/21/2631298

CHAPTER FOUR

The power of yet: Carol S Dweck: TED Conference. YouTube. (2014, September 12). Retrieved October 28, 2022, from https://youtu.be/J-swZaKN2Ic

FutureLearn. (2022, April 25). What is a growth mindset and how can you develop one? FutureLearn. Retrieved October 28, 2022, from https://www.futurelearn.com/info/blog/general/develop-growth-mindset

Fensterwald, J. (2015, November 23). There's more to a 'growth mindset' than assuming you have it. EdSource. Retrieved October 28, 2022, from https://edsource.org/2015/theres-more-to-a-growth-mindset-than-assuming-you-have-it/

Growth Mindset vs. fixed mindset: What's the difference? Business Insights Blog. (2022, March 10). Retrieved October 28, 2022, from https://online.hbs.edu/blog/post/growth-mindset-vs-fixed-mindset

Fixed and growth mindset. FutureLearn. (n.d.). Retrieved October 28, 2022, from https://www.futurelearn.com/info/courses/improving-study-techniques/0/steps/55541

Growth mindset vs fixed mindset: How what you think affects what you achieve. Mindset Health. (n.d.). Retrieved October 28, 2022, from https://www.mindsethealth.com/matter/growth-vs-fixed-mindset

Rapier, G. (n.d.). Steve Ballmer famously slammed the iphone - here are 12 other times bosses got it wrong on new tech. Business Insider. Retrieved October 28, 2022, from https://www.businessinsider.com/iphone-steve-ballmer-bosses-mocked-new-technologyand-got-it-wrong-2017-6

Growth Mindset In Major Companies And Resilience - CTR training. (n.d.). Retrieved October 28, 2022, from https://ctrtraining.co.uk/documents/Resilience-GPUpdate.pdf

CHAPTER FIVE

10 ways to increase your emotional intelligence | inc.com. (n.d.). Retrieved October 28, 2022, from https://www.inc.com/young-entrepreneur-council/10-ways-to-increase-your-emotional-intelligence.html

Lebow, H. I. (2021, June 7). Emotional intelligence (EQ). Psych Central. Retrieved October 28, 2022, from https://psychcentral.com/lib/what-is-emotional-intelligence-eq#examples

L;, R. P. N. J. O. (n.d.). IQ scores among homeless older adolescents: Characteristics of intellectual performance and associations with psychosocial functioning. Journal of adolescence. Retrieved October 28, 2022, from https://pubmed.ncbi.nlm.nih.gov/10462423/

León-Del-Barco, B., Lázaro, S. M., Polo-Del-Río, M.-I., & López-Ramos, V.-M. (2020, December 15). Emotional intelligence as a protective factor against victimization in school bullying. International journal of environmental research and public health. Retrieved October 28, 2022, from https://www.ncbi.nlm.nih.gov/pmc/articles/PMC7765427/

León-Pérez, J. M., Cantero-Sánchez, F. J., Fernández-Canseco, Á., & León-Rubio, J. M. (2021, October 24). Effectiveness of a humor-based training for reducing employees' distress. International journal of environmental research and public health. Retrieved October 28, 2022, from https://www.ncbi.nlm.nih.gov/pmc/articles/PMC8583317/

CHAPTER SIX

Functional Medicine Coaching Academy. (2021, May 14). Brain detox: Is it time for a cleanse? Functional Medicine Coaching Academy. Retrieved October 28, 2022, from https://functionalmedicinecoaching.org/brain-detox-is-it-time-for-a-cleanse/

Matt Walker on why sleep is your superpower. What We Seee. (2020, May 4). Retrieved September 16, 2022, from https://www.whatweseee.com/matt-walker-sleep/

REM sleep's role in Creative Solutions, Dream Inspiration and Wisdom: Matthew Walker. FoundMyFitness. (n.d.). Retrieved October 28, 2022, from https://www.foundmyfitness.com/episodes/rem-sleep-creative-solutions-dream-inspiration-wisdom

Contributors, W. M. D. E. (n.d.). Caffeine: How long do its effects last? WebMD. Retrieved September 16, 2022, from https://www.webmd.com/diet/how-long-caffeine-lasts

Saletin, J. M., Goldstein, A. N., & Walker, M. P. (2011, November). The role of sleep in directed forgetting and remembering of human memories. Cerebral cortex (New York, N.Y. : 1991).

Retrieved October 28, 2022, from https://www.ncbi.nlm.nih.gov/pmc/articles/PMC3183424/

60minutes. (2018, January 10). 60 Minutes: Brain hacking. YouTube. Retrieved October 28, 2022, from https://youtube.com/watch?v=awAMTQZmvPE

Achieving brain clearance and preventing neurodegenerative diseases—a ... (n.d.). Retrieved October 28, 2022, from https://journals.sagepub.com/doi/10.1177/0271678X20982388

G;, N. A. D. J. L. D. (n.d.). Caffeine and the central nervous system: Mechanisms of action, biochemical, metabolic and psychostimulant effects. Brain research. Brain research reviews. Retrieved October 28, 2022, from https://pubmed.ncbi.nlm.nih.gov/1356551

REM sleep's role in Creative Solutions, Dream Inspiration and Wisdom: Matthew Walker. FoundMyFitness. (n.d.). Retrieved October 28, 2022, from https://www.foundmyfitness.com/episodes/rem-sleep-creative-solutions-dream-inspiration-wisdom

Huguet, M., Payne, J. D., Kim, S. Y., & Alger, S. E. (2019, August 29). Overnight sleep benefits both neutral and negative direct associative and relational memory - cognitive, affective, & behavioral neuroscience. SpringerLink. Retrieved October 28, 2022, from https://link.springer.com/article/10.3758/s13415-019-00746-8

Saletin, J. M., Goldstein, A. N., & Walker, M. P. (2011, November). The role of sleep in directed forgetting and remembering of human memories. Cerebral cortex (New York, N.Y. : 1991). Retrieved October 28, 2022, from https://www.ncbi.nlm.nih.gov/pmc/articles/PMC3183424/

Track your sleep with Apple Watch. Apple Support. (n.d.). Retrieved September 16, 2022, from https://support.apple.com/guide/watch/sleep-apd830528336/watchos

CHAPTER SEVEN

Benefits of mindfulness. HelpGuide.org. (n.d.). Retrieved October 28, 2022, from https://www.helpguide.org/harvard/benefits-of-mindfulness.htm

Wikimedia Foundation. (2017, July 7). Talk:maharishi Mahesh Yogi/consciousness. Wikipedia. Retrieved October 28, 2022, from https://en.wikipedia.org/wiki/Talk%3AMaharishi_Mahesh_Yogi%2FConsciousness

Buddha's brain - amazon.com. (n.d.). Retrieved October 28, 2022, from https://www.amazon.com/Buddhas-Brain-Practical-Neuroscience-Happiness/dp/1491518669

6 steps to mindfulness meditation. Live Happy. (n.d.). Retrieved October 28, 2022, from https://www.livehappy.com/practice/6-steps-to-mindfulness-meditation

Davidson, R. J. (n.d.). How mindfulness changes the emotional life of our brains: Richard J. Davidson: Tedxsanfrancisco. Richard J. Davidson: How mindfulness changes the emotional life of our brains | Richard J. Davidson | TEDxSanFrancisco | TED Talk. Retrieved October 28, 2022, from https://www.ted.com/talks/richard_j_davidson_how_mindfulness_changes_the_emotional_life_of_our_brains_jan_2019

Powell, A. (2018, August 27). Harvard researchers study how mindfulness may change the brain in depressed patients. Harvard Gazette. Retrieved October 28, 2022, from https://news.harvard.edu/gazette/story/2018/04/harvard-researchers-study-how-mindfulness-may-change-the-brain-in-depressed-patients/

U.S. Department of Health and Human Services. (n.d.). Meditation and mindfulness: What you need to know. National Center for

Complementary and Integrative Health. Retrieved October 28, 2022, from https://www.nccih.nih.gov/health/meditation-and-mindfulness-what-you-need-to-know

Brady, A. (2021, August 27). 4 advanced meditation techniques and tools to deepen your practice. Chopra. Retrieved October 28, 2022, from https://chopra.com/articles/4-advanced-meditation-techniques-and-tools-to-deepen-your-practice

MediLexicon International. (n.d.). 4-7-8 breathing: How it works, benefits, and uses. Medical News Today. Retrieved October 28, 2022, from https://www.medicalnewstoday.com/articles/324417#benefits

CHAPTER EIGHT

Encyclopædia Britannica, inc. (n.d.). Napoleon summary. Encyclopædia Britannica. Retrieved October 28, 2022, from https://www.britannica.com/summary/Napoleon-I

Encyclopædia Britannica, inc. (n.d.). Napoleonic wars summary. Encyclopædia Britannica. Retrieved October 28, 2022, from https://www.britannica.com/summary/Napoleonic-Wars

Why is strategic planning important?: HBS Online. Business Insights Blog. (2020, October 6). Retrieved October 28, 2022, from https://online.hbs.edu/blog/post/why-is-strategic-planning-important

4 ways to develop your strategic thinking skills: HBS Online. Business Insights Blog. (2020, September 10). Retrieved October 28, 2022, from https://online.hbs.edu/blog/post/how-to-develop-strategic-thinking-skills

Marieforleo. (2019, September 13). Self-made millionaire: The simple strategy that helped increase my odds of success by 42%. CNBC. Retrieved October 28, 2022, from https://www.cnbc.com/2019/09/13/self-made-millionaire-how-to-increase-your-odds-of-success-by-42-percent-marie-forleo.html

Elle Kaplan. (2017, November 21). 3 smart habits that will improve your wealth and success this month. Elle Kaplan. Retrieved October 28, 2022, from https://ellekaplan.com/3-smart-habits-will-improve-wealth-success-month/

Elle Kaplan. (2017, August 22). 3 behaviors that will put you on the path to Success. Elle Kaplan. Retrieved October 28, 2022, from https://ellekaplan.com/3-behaviors-will-put-path-success/

Elle Kaplan. (2017, August 22). 3 behaviors that will put you on the path to Success. Elle Kaplan. Retrieved October 28, 2022, from https://ellekaplan.com/3-behaviors-will-put-path-success/

CHAPTER NINE

Hogan, C. (2020, April 30). How to switch out of your default mode and live from your advanced settings. Medium. Retrieved October 28, 2022, from https://medium.com/@cchogan1/how-to-switch-out-of-your-default-mode-and-live-from-your-advanced-settings-d59b64a55a23

Getaway. (2020, July 7). Read about the default mode network: Getaway. Getaway Journal. Retrieved October 28, 2022, from https://journal.getaway.house/default-mode-network-your-mind-at-rest/

Haddadeen, S. (2022, September 24). Psilocybin and the default mode network. Microdose. Retrieved October 28, 2022, from https://www.microdosebros.com/psilocybin-and-the-default-mode-network/#:

Li, W., Mai, X., & Liu, C. (1AD, January 1). The default mode network and social understanding of others: What do brain connectivity studies tell us. Frontiers. Retrieved October 28, 2022, from https://www.frontiersin.org/articles/10.3389/fnhum.2014.00074/full

Forster, P. (2021, June 24). Default mode network and depression treatment - ketamine and TMS. Gateway Psychiatric. Retrieved

October 28, 2022, from https://www.gatewaypsychiatric.com/default-mode-network-and-depression/

Koselka, E. P. D., Weidner, L. C., Minasov, A., Berman, M. G., Leonard, W. R., Santoso, M. V., de Brito, J. N., Pope, Z. C., Pereira, M. A., & Horton, T. H. (2019, November 7). Walking green: Developing an evidence base for nature prescriptions. International journal of environmental research and public health. Retrieved October 28, 2022, from https://www.ncbi.nlm.nih.gov/pmc/articles/PMC6888434/

Akiki TJ;Averill CL;Wrocklage KM;Scott JC;Averill LA;Schweinsburg B;Alexander-Bloch A;Martini B;Southwick SM;Krystal JH;Abdallah CG; (n.d.). Default mode network abnormalities in posttraumatic stress disorder: A novel network-restricted topology approach. NeuroImage. Retrieved October 28, 2022, from https://pubmed.ncbi.nlm.nih.gov/29730491/

Kirchner, B. (2018, July 18). TPN vs. DMN - neural mechanisms and mindfulness. Exploring The Business Brain. Retrieved October 28, 2022, from https://exploringthebusinessbrain.com/tpn-vs-dmn-neural-mechanisms-mindfulness/

CHAPTER TEN

WebMD. (n.d.). Famous people with ADHD / ADD: 13 celebrities with ADHD / add. WebMD. Retrieved October 28, 2022, from https://www.webmd.com/add-adhd/ss/slideshow-celebrities-add-adhd

Holland, K. (2020, March 25). Celebrities with ADHD: 9 famous people with ADHD. Healthline. Retrieved October 28, 2022, from https://www.healthline.com/health/adhd/celebrities#1.-Michael-Phelps

Holland, K. (2020, March 25). Celebrities with ADHD: 9 famous people with ADHD. Healthline. Retrieved October 28, 2022, from https://www.healthline.com/health/adhd/celebrities

Kernbach, J. M., Satterthwaite, T. D., Bassett, D. S., Smallwood, J., Margulies, D., Krall, S., Shaw, P., Varoquaux, G., Thirion, B., Konrad, K., & Bzdok, D. (2018, July 17). Shared endo-phenotypes of default mode dysfunction in attention deficit/hyperactivity disorder and autism spectrum disorder. Nature News. Retrieved October 28, 2022, from https://www.nature.com/articles/s41398-018-0179-6

What is ADHD? Psychiatry.org - What is ADHD? (n.d.). Retrieved October 28, 2022, from https://www.psychiatry.org/patients-families/adhd/what-is-adhd

Fox, K. C. R., Nijeboer, S., Dixon, M. L., Floman, J. L., Ellamil, M., Rumak, S. P., Sedlmeier, P., & Christoff, K. (2014, April 3). Is meditation associated with altered brain structure? A systematic review and meta-analysis of morphometric neuroimaging in meditation practitioners. Neuroscience & Biobehavioral Reviews. Retrieved October 28, 2022, from https://www.sciencedirect.com/science/article/pii/S01497634 14000724

NHS. (n.d.). ADHD Diagnosis. NHS choices. Retrieved October 28, 2022, from https://www.nhs.uk/conditions/attention-deficit-hyperactivity-disorder-adhd/diagnosis/

Schimelpfening, N. (2022, July 23). Dialectical behavior therapy (DBT): Definition, techniques, and efficacy. Verywell Mind. Retrieved October 28, 2022, from https://www.verywellmind.com/dialectical-behavior-therapy-1067402

Kasuya-Ueba, Y., Zhao, S., & Toichi, M. (1AD, January 1). The effect of music intervention on attention in children: Experimental evidence. Frontiers. Retrieved October 28, 2022, from https://www.frontiersin.org/articles/10.3389/fnins.2020.00757/full

Benefits of Music for General Public. Listen4Life Foundation. (n.d.). Retrieved October 28, 2022, from https://www.listenforlife.org/healing-benefits.html

Kollins, D. S. (n.d.). Video-game therapy may help treat ADHD, study finds. ABC News. Retrieved October 28, 2022, from https://abcnews.go.com/Health/video-game-therapy-treat-adhd-study-finds/story?id=69186285

Is therapy using horses effective for ADHD? CHADD. (2019, February 28). Retrieved October 28, 2022, from https://chadd.org/adhd-weekly/is-therapy-using-horses-effective-for-adhd/

Boddy-Evans, M. (2019, February 20). The effect of "Right brain left brain" on art. LiveAbout. Retrieved October 28, 2022, from https://www.liveabout.com/right-brain-left-brain-theory-art-2579156

Kasuya-Ueba, Y., Zhao, S., & Toichi, M. (1AD, January 1). The effect of music intervention on attention in children: Experimental evidence. Frontiers. Retrieved October 28, 2022, from https://www.frontiersin.org/articles/10.3389/fnins.2020.00757/full

WebMD. (n.d.). Proceed with caution: 10 things you should consider before stopping your ADHD meds. WebMD. Retrieved October 28, 2022, from https://www.webmd.com/add-adhd/ss/cm/10-things-you-should-consider-before-stopping-adhd-meds

CLOSING THOUGHTS

Xplore. (n.d.). Walt Disney quotes. BrainyQuote. Retrieved October 28, 2022, from https://www.brainyquote.com/quotes/walt_disney_163027